TOWPAT

The South Oxford Canal

Nick Corble

First published 2005

Tempus Publishing Limited
The Mill, Brimscombe Port,
Stroud, Gloucestershire, GL5 2QG

© Nick Corble, 2005

The right of Nick Corble to be identified as the Author
of this work has been asserted in accordance with the
Copyrights, Designs and Patents Act 1988.

All rights reserved. No part of this book may be reprinted
or reproduced or utilised in any form or by any electronic,
mechanical or other means, now known or hereafter invented,
including photocopying and recording, or in any information
storage or retrieval system, without the permission in writing
from the Publishers.

British Library Cataloguing in Publication Data.
A catalogue record for this book is available from the British Library.

ISBN 0 7524 3536 1

Typesetting and design by Liz Rudderham
Origination by Tempus Publishing Limited
Printed and bound in Great Britain

CONTENTS

INTRODUCTION

The renaissance of the canals towards the latter part of the last century was one of the country's greatest, but largely unsung, success stories. A major new leisure resource emerged that somehow managed to bring together our collective love of the countryside, our pride in our past and our growing need for an escape from the fast pace of modern living. There is no doubt about it; the canals, once in danger of being filled in and erased from history, are here to stay.

Perhaps the most distinguishing feature of our canal system is the boats that ply their way slowly but steadily through it. However, although boaters clearly represent the most visible group of canal users, they are by no means the only ones to appreciate their worth. It has been estimated that over 400 million visits are made to the canal system each year, only 2 million of which are by boaters.

The reality is that the canals have become more than simply a transport system; they have evolved into visitor corridors. Walkers, riders, anglers, cyclists or simply those amongst the half of the population who live within 5 miles of an inland waterway, now regularly pass through these corridors. Cyclists alone account for three times as many visits as boaters and the total number to utilise the canals is expected to double over the coming decade.

These new Guides have been written to reflect this burgeoning reality. They will appeal to boaters but will also reach out beyond them to these other groups – the backpacker planning a towpath walk, motorists looking to spend long weekends staying in bed and breakfasts, riders looking to discover the joy of towpath routes... the list goes on.

The Guides have been prepared to inform, amuse and spark an interest in the areas surrounding the canals, with the visitor corridor being defined as spanning roughly 2 miles either side of the towpath. Anecdotes and interesting facts are scattered throughout to provide colour and bring these areas alive to the reader. Only the most resilient are likely to resist the temptation to repeat at least some of these to their companions.

For ease of use, each canal is broken down into sections covering between 7-12 miles, with sections themselves broken down into the following four groupings:

SHAPERS

Describing the route of the canal, the local history associated with it and details of the natural landscape and transport links, this section provides the basic background to each section.

BASICS

Where to shop, find a pub or locate a place to stay as well as places to eat. All these topics are covered here, taking the sting out of finding your way around and the essentials of getting by.

SEEING AND DOING

What to look out for and where it's worth making a diversion to see that oddity or curiosity you might not otherwise find, plus where to find that something a bit special culturally or where to go if you simply want to be entertained.

SAMPLING

Ways to dip into the local area and become part of the landscape, whether you are walking or cycling (a recommended route is provide for both in each section), riding, fishing or want to wander around a golf course.

Each section is accompanied by maps which allow users to pinpoint where the places mentioned sit within the corridor. Phone numbers and websites are given as appropriate and the 'Learn More and Links' section provides pointers on where to look if you want to follow up on items covered in the Guide – making it simple if you want to check a pub's opening hours, whether a leisure centre has a squash court or the times of a local bus.

We hope that these new Guides will encourage more people to enjoy our inland waterways and help to deepen their appreciation of the symbiotic relationship between the canals and the towns and villages that surround them.

Nick Corble
Series Editor

NOTE: *Cyclists need a permit from British Waterways – either apply direct or download one from their website www.britishwaterways.co.uk. Likewise, anglers should check who controls fishing rights on particular stretches and details are provided in the sampling sections.*

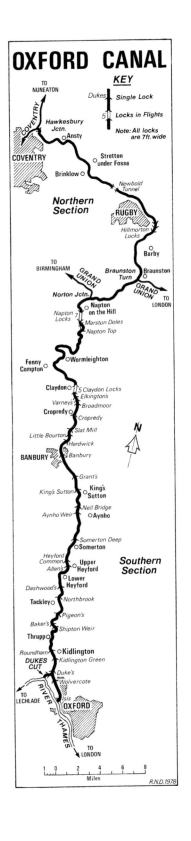

OXFORD CANAL

KEY

Dukes ▮ Single Lock

5 ▮ Locks in Flights

Note: All locks are 7ft. wide

TO NUNEATON

COVENTRY

Hawkesbury Jctn.
Ansty

COVENTRY

Stretton under Fosse

Brinklow

Newbold Tunnel

Northern Section

RUGBY

Hillmorton Locks

Barby

TO BIRMINGHAM

GRAND UNION

Braunston Turn — Braunston

GRAND UNION

TO LONDON

Norton Jctn.

Napton on the Hill

Napton Locks 7

Marston Doles

Napton Top

Fenny Compton

Wormleighton

Claydon — 5 Claydon Locks
Elkington's
Varney's — Broadmoor
Cropredy
Cropredy
Slat Mill
Little Bourton
Hardwick
BANBURY — Banbury

Grant's

King's Sutton — King's Sutton

Nell Bridge
Aynho Weir — Aynho

Somerton Deep
Somerton

Heyford Common
Allen's — Upper Heyford

Lower Heyford

Dashwood's
Tackley — Northbrook

Pigeon's

Baker's
Shipton Weir
Thrupp

Roundham — Kidlington
Kidlington Green

DUKES CUT
Duke's
Wolvercote

TO LECHLADE

RIVER THAMES

Isis
OXFORD

TO LONDON

Southern Section

N

1 0 2 4 6 8
Miles

R.N.D.1978

OVERVIEW

The Oxford Canal is many people's favourite. Sandwiched between the more urban delights of the Birmingham Navigations to the north and the grandeur of Old Father Thames to the south, it occupies a unique piece in the jigsaw that is the canal network. Originally part of the canal pioneer James Brindley's 'Grand Cross', linking the four great eighteenth-century seaports of Hull, London, Bristol and Liverpool, the Oxford's role was to provide the link to London via the Thames.

It achieved this by linking up with the Coventry Canal, which in turn joined up with the Trent and Mersey. In so doing, it also provided a means of transporting Midlands coal to Banbury and Oxford and a way of moving finished goods out of these places to practically anywhere in the country. When the first barge laden with coal arrived at New Road Wharf in Oxford on 1 January 1790 it was met with enthusiasm and the rousing sound of the Oxford Militia Band.

> Fuel had become a real problem for this part of the country. So much wood had been chopped down during the Civil War, that many were forced to burn straw for warmth during the winter months.

The canal's heyday was a short one though. These days the Oxford Canal is split into two, the North

> The Oxford Canal cost a total of £280,000 to build.

and South, and the reason for this divide is also the reason why the canal never really fully realised the aspirations its backers originally set for it. Only eleven years after it opened a more reliable route between the Midlands and London was opened with what is known today as the Grand Union Canal.

This route was not only faster and easier to negotiate, but it also threw into stark relief the basic deficiencies of the canal. Wanting nothing but the best, the men behind the Oxford Canal commissioned James Brindley, the man who effectively invented canal building in this country, but the relationship between them was never an easy one. In fact, in the canal's early days Brindley was given the sack because it was felt he wasn't devoting enough time to the canal, but in the absence of an alternative the Committee had to write a grovelling apology to get him back.

Brindley died before the canal really got going but before he went he had time to set out a route. This was to prove crucial to forming the canal as we know it today, as the great man was well known for his aversion to building locks unless they were strictly necessary, leading to the practice of 'hugging the contour', passing round a rise in the land rather than up and over or even through it.

The net effect of Brindley's plan was a canal that twists and turns like a wayward mooring rope. One stretch around Wormleighton can still take half a day to negotiate in order to achieve less than a mile as the crow flies.

It was this inefficiency that the canal's rival exploited. The new route was not only quicker, but it avoided the need to travel along the Thames, a waterway that remained hazardous and unpredictable, and worst of all was even tidal for a while. Whilst the Oxford Canal Company was still paying a dividend of 23 per cent in 1829, within fifty years this had dwindled to less than 4 per cent.

> In 1714 the River Thames was so low that people could cross it without getting their feet wet. Even by 1793 boats were taking up to eight weeks to get from London to Oxford.

> Oxfordshire's economy suffered badly during the late nineteenth and early twentieth century – from one of the richest counties in the kingdom it became one of the poorest. By 1911 the county's farm workers were the lowest paid in the country.

Whilst attempts were made to make the canal more efficient, including a programme of 'straightenings' in the northern section, which loped 14 miles off the original 36-mile route, the ever-present talk of yet more rivals being built to tap the few markets where the canal could earn its keep made it hard to justify further investment.

What kept the canal alive during the nineteenth century was what became known as the 'golden 6 miles', the stretch that linked the waterway's northern and southern sections. As luck would have it this constituted part of the Grand Union route and the canal's owners had no qualms about charging exorbitant tolls for the use of this modest stretch of its water.

With its links into Coventry the northern section of the canal was more viable, and in the middle of the twentieth century the southern section was lucky to survive at all. The New Road Wharf was filled in and the site sold to Nuffield College in 1937. Commercial traffic ceased in the 1950s and at one time there were plans to build a bus station on land occupied by the canal in Banbury.

It was the defeat of these plans that effectively reversed the fortunes of the canal. A rally on the proposed bus station site led to the

An angler with his catch, Boddington.

formation of the Inland Waterways Association and a voice for those who saw a future for the canals. The leisure age was born.

Perhaps ironically, it is the very features that made the canal so uneconomical nearly 200 years ago that help make it so popular to the

A typical Oxford lift bridge. Most are left open these days.

modern user. This Guide covers the South Oxford Canal, from Napton with its windmill staring down on the canal in the north, to Oxford and the Thames in the south.

Covering just under 50 miles, the canal passes through parts of rural England that it would be easy to think had been lost forever as it describes a broad north to south route towards its final destination. Its circuitous route is now seen as less of a burden and part of its charm, with every bend offering the potential of something new.

Although the canal has its fair share of traditional stone hump-backed bridges, the fact that the canal's builders were constantly short of money led to a profusion of much cheaper wooden lift bridges. Once again, something that contributed to the canal's inefficiency is today seen as one of its greatest assets, with these bridges now recognised as a hallmark.

The South Oxford Canal starts in the southern reaches of Warwickshire, and for a brief while flirts with the idea of visiting Northamptonshire before easing its way into the northern tip of Oxfordshire at Banbury. This point marks a rough halfway point and a critical one, for it is around here that it is joined by its near-constant companion for the rest of the journey: the River Cherwell, whose valley it shares.

The villages to the north of Banbury are characterised by the distinctive orange/brown hue of the local ironstone. Dispersed but distinct, each has their own history and character, with secrets to be unearthed. As the canal wends its way in a vague southerly direction it passes by the village of Claydon, with its Bygones Museum offering a chance to touch and see how rural life progressed during the last century. A little further on the canal passes along the edge of the historic village of Cropredy, famous for its annual folk music festival but also the site of a Civil War skirmish. A village whose fortunes were revived by the arrival of the canal, Cropredy had a brickworks and toll house where a beam would fall across the water and rise again only when the requisite fee had been paid.

As has already been mentioned, Banbury represents one of the few real towns on this largely rural canal. Indeed, the successful traveller down this visitor corridor will need to learn the art of planning ahead, for this is not a canal blessed with regular services. The area's rural heritage was recognised after the Second World War when Banbury was chosen as the location for a Government film that summarised how country-folk made their living.

The canal seems to unravel after Banbury, passing through the Heyfords and close to a series of other small villages before joining up with the Cherwell through a section known as The Wides, a delightful stretch of reed-lined banks and wide water, with the added adventure of a current. Next up is the archetypal canal village of Thrupp after which the route clips the edge of Kidlington – officially the largest village in Britain.

After here it's a contented slide down into Oxford, where the canal nestles on the edge of the city, and a fitting conclusion to the journey. Such is the modern success of the canal that plans are now afoot to open up the original New Road Wharf Basin – a clear case of turning back the tide.

The South Oxford Canal is a box of delights waiting to be opened. We hope this Guide will help you unwrap it.

This sign on the engine of a traditional narrow-boat sums up the attraction of the canals.

SECTION A
Napton Junction to Fenny Compton

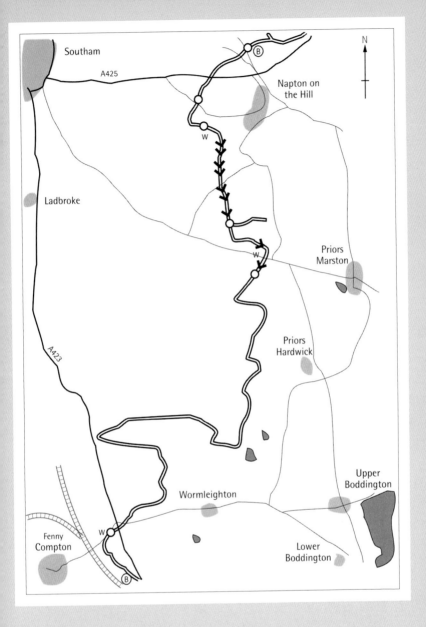

Southam

A425

Ladbroke

A423

Napton on
the Hill

Priors
Marston

Priors
Hardwick

Upper
Boddington

Wormleighton

W

Fenny
Compton

B

Lower
Boddington

N

W

W

Key

—— Canal
.... River
▦▦▦▦ Railway
– – Motorway
—— A Road
— B Road

◖ Built up area
◗ Stations
◗ Open water

◯ Turning point
⋀ Lock
Ⓑ Boatyard
W Waterpoint

SHAPERS

THE CANAL ON THIS STRETCH

KEY FACTS

LENGTH: 11.25 miles

BOATYARDS: 2
>   Napton
>   Fenny Compton

WATERPOINTS: 3
>   Napton
>   Marston Doles
>   Fenny Compton Wharf

NB: Water is also available to customers of the two boatyards.

TURNING POINTS: 6
>   Napton Junction
>   Napton Boatyard
>   Napton
>   Old Engine House Arm
>   Marston Doles – 50ft only
>   Fenny Compton Wharf

NB: Turning is not allowed at Fenny Compton Boatyard, which is separate from the Wharf.

LOCKS: 9
>   Napton Flight (49ft 1in)

This section links the only two real centres of population near the canal, Napton and Fenny Compton, although both lie some distance from the water. This is a very rural stretch and not one boaters will wish to contemplate if they are in a hurry as the twists and turns that distinguish it can be extremely frustrating with landmarks lingering rather than fading. By way of contrast, these very features make it convenient for walkers and cyclists to construct circular tours.

For the purposes of this Guide the beginning of the South Oxford Canal is taken to be Napton Junction, with the stretch linking it to its northern counterpart at Braunston *de facto* (if not necessarily *de jure*) part of the Grand Union. A broad sweep follows after the Junction

The view through Folly Bridge at Napton.

with Napton Marina on the non-towpath side. Accessible from bridges 109 to 112, the towpath here is fine for walking, if a little bumpy for cyclists.

From Bridge 111 it becomes apparent that the canal is skirting the base of the looming Napton Hill, with geese usually taking advantage of the grass hereabouts. As its name suggests, Napton on the Hill sits proudly above the water and is best accessed from Bridge 113, a fact reflected in the stretch of 14-day, and then 48-hour moorings along the run-up to the bridge. Just before the moorings there is also a turning point. In the summer months it can get very busy here and boaters may be advised to take what they can.

The Folly Pie Pub is well advertised with claims that it is the last public house for five hours, with the canal entering a very rural stretch after this point. The moorings run out suddenly the other side of a sharp bend where there is a water point and sanitary station. The flight itself is made up of single locks with plenty of space between them for passing. The first four follow in quick succession, with only a short pause before two more. Look out for the felled pylons in the fields either side of lock 13, after which there is a sharp bend to the left and then another, less acute bend to the right by a concrete pillbox.

The landscape hereabouts is flat, with cows and sheep grazing quietly in the fields. There is a slight rise to the east and on a clear day Napton's hill and windmill behind you continue to dominate the skyline. A track up from Holt's Farm allows access to the water with boats moored by the Old Engine Arm a short walk down from Napton Adkin's Lock (Number 14).

Some regard this as the end of the Napton Flight, classifying the two that follow after a wide sweep in which the canal doubles back on itself as the Marston Doles Locks. Either way, a 50ft turning point and water point the other side of the second of these announce that this is the end of locking for a while, for the canal is about to enter its summit, a fact confirmed by the presence of an old pump house by the side of the Top Lock.

The canal is now level with the surrounding countryside, although a high hedge along the towpath hides just how much it is hugging the contour, with the field behind the hedge sloping gently downwards. The towpath remains solid, following a long, straight south-westerly path for half a mile. Mooring remains good, although not universally so, with some reinforced banks when the canal does finally curve round. There are good views to be had to the west here through a rare gap in the hedge.

The water bends round before resuming its south-westerly route after Bridge 122, but from this point any natural sense of direction is seriously challenged as the canal staggers a vague course south like a drunk, showing only an occasional moment of lucidity. Good moorings follow Bridge 124 although the hedge continues to hide the view. By way of compensation, the hills to the east edge their way up to the water to give a bit of profile.

After Bridge 126 the canal diverts to the west with a couple of bends by a farm. Just after these a gap in the hedge looks back to this bridge, suggesting a serious lack of progress. The towpath becomes less friendly here although the view opens out again after Bridge 128 onto the Warwickshire flatlands. There is good mooring between Bridges 129 and

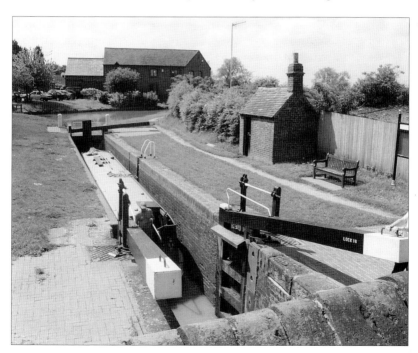

Marston Doles and the last of the Napton Flight.

130 and again the other side of Bridge 131. Many of the bends along this stretch are reinforced with steel and little wonder, considering the wash that must be thrown up by some of the boats negotiating them!

Two more straight sections linked by one such sharp bend precede Bridge 134, with the bank between the next two bridges reserved for moorings, graduating down from long term through 14 day to 48 hour, with the latter giving good access to the excellent Wharf Inn. After the bridge there is a turning point and water, followed by more moorings which reverse the previous pattern, ending with long term all the way through to the Cowroast or Fenny Compton Marina (01295 770934).

PRINCIPAL TOWNS AND VILLAGES ALONG THIS STRETCH

FENNY COMPTON
A scattered village which exists independently of the canal with evidence of continuing farming as well as more modern commercial enterprises. It also has the impressive partly fourteenth-century church of St Peter and (unusually) St Clare on top of a hill. The name 'fenny' means wetland and refers to the fact that the village was subject to flooding from the Burton Dassett hills to the south, and even today a flood marker guards the bridge under the railway to the north of the village.

> In June 2003 a syndicate of seven from a manufacturer of concrete buildings in Fenny Compton scooped nearly £2 million on the National Lottery draw.

LADBROKE
Set off the A423, Ladbroke stands alone between Fenny Compton and Southam with open countryside to the north and south. Black and white half-timbered houses reminiscent of Stratford lie to the west,

> Ladbroke Manor was once owned by the Gunpowder Plot conspirator Robert Catesby. The village has also been home to the car maker Lord Rootes and the founders of the bookmakers Ladbrokes, who named their firm after the village.

reminding the visitor that they are now in Warwickshire. The village has a long history, pre-dating the Conquest, when the population was around 250, about the same as it is today.

Ladbroke Millennium Stone with the church in the background.

NAPTON

The name Napton translates from the Celtic to mean 'the farm in the knap of the hill', with the hill its defining feature, along with the windmill which sits on top of it and dates back to 1543. It is now privately owned. With a population of around 1,000 spread out over the hill and down its sides, Napton is one of the few villages to support more than one pub along this stretch. The chestnut tree on the village green was planted to mark the coronation of King George V, and the Butts leading up to St Lawrence's church is named after the furlong strip farming that was in use here from Saxon times until the enclosures.

> Stones to build St Lawrence's church were left at the bottom of the hill where the church was to be built, but overnight they appeared on the top of the hill so the locals quite sensibly took this as a sign and built the church where it stands today.

PRIORS HARDWICK

Once a thriving medieval village, Priors Hardwick was decimated by the effects first of the plague and then the sheep enclosures and was partly demolished by Cistercian monks in the fourteenth century. These days it seems to be thriving once again, with the elegant Butcher's Arms restaurant a big draw. St Mary's church, just up from the pub, has an impressive lychgate, built in 1862 to celebrate Queen Victoria's Jubilee, and the village still has its own public tap.

PRIORS MARSTON

A dispersed village with a mix of building styles and still plenty of building activity, with the distinctive local brown stone much in evidence. As its name suggests, along with Priors Hardwick, the village was once owned by the Priors of Coventry, passing to the Spencer family after the Dissolution. The village also has an unusual War Memorial. To the west of Priors Marston on the old Welsh Road lies Marston Doles, which today is little more than a couple of houses and some offices by the canal.

> The Welsh Road is so named because it was used by sheep farmers from Wales, who drove their sheep to London along this route to avoid the tolls on other, more traditional routes.

SOUTHAM

Ordinarily, Southam would be regarded as a small market town with a compact centre and a sprawl of modern housing on its outskirts. It is these things, but it is also the main shopping centre on this stretch and offers a surprising mix of historical buildings and connections. It has had its own town market since Henry III granted it a charter

> Southam is mentioned in Shakespeare's *Henry VI Part 3* as the place where Warwick the Kingmaker's ally Clarence has gathered his forces.

in 1227 and like the two Priors, Hardwick and Marston, was for a time owned by the Priors of Coventry.

UPPER BODDINGTON
Triangulated by three farms, Upper Boddington's highlights are concentrated into a small area which includes the church of St John the Baptist, a primary school and a small shop, with the village 'local' the Plough also nearby.

WORMLEIGHTON
Although the church here dates from the twelfth century, the village was effectively deserted at the end of the fifteenth century, with evidence of the original housing still evident in the bumps and hillocks in the local landscape. The Manor was built later by Robert Spencer, including the Gatehouse on the south front which sports the rose and thistle of the Royal Arms. Today there is a scattering of houses, including both the manor and Wormleighton Hall.

> The man responsible for the sheep enclosures that led to Wormleighton's demise was William Cope, who was also keeper of King Henry VII's coffers.

HISTORY

The absence of any natural centre along this stretch, coupled with the reliance on farming to make a living, meant that for centuries those living here were able to develop their own communities in the way they thought best until external influences intervened.

Evidence of ridge and furrow farming suggests that most of the settlements in this area can date themselves back beyond Saxon times, when they were probably little more than collections of families who together scraped a living from the soil. Archaeology has also revealed a number of examples of early settlement, including the ruins of a Stone Age defensive fortress on Grendenton Hill to the west of Fenny Compton and Roman coins in and around Southam.

But by the time of the Domesday Book in 1086 even Southam was recorded as having only four hides, with a hide defined as sufficient land to support a family. In addition there were two water mills and some woods, as well as enough arable land to support twelve ploughs. A total population of around 170 was distributed amongst thirty-five families, many of which were peasants and bondsmen. Then as now, Southam would not have been typical of local centres of population, its position at the confluence of local transport routes and the natural advantage of lying on the River Stowe marking it out as exceptional.

It is around this time that the first of those external influences began to have an impact. The Norman Conquest resulted in a re-parcelling of the land and many of the families that had built up local power and prestige discovered the price of backing the loser in a war. A good

Upper Boddington.

example of this is Fenny Compton, which before the Conquest had been dominated by five large local families. One of these, the Turchil family who had had the foresight to back the invader, was rewarded with the lands of the other four.

This and similar developments meant the creation of sufficient blocks of land to support manor houses, which either stayed within a family or, in time, passed to the Church, with both Priors Marston and Priors Hardwick becoming the property of the Prior of Coventry, along with Southam, although in this case the Priory had received the settlement from Leofric, the husband of Lady Godiva, just before the Conquest in 1047. The Priory at Clattercote to the south also owned much of the land around modern Fenny Compton.

For the next 500 years this feudal model dominated, with many more manors existing than there are villages today, with the area to the south of modern Warwickshire being known as 'Feldon'. During this time Napton grew to be one of the largest settlements in Warwickshire, with a population of around 1,000 in 1400, roughly the same as it is today.

The reason why so many of these settlements have disappeared is the second major *deus ex machina* to affect the area, the movement to enclose common land, including that used for grazing sheep which, which combined with the Dissolution of the Monasteries and subsequent shift in the local power base, led to dramatic changes in the local landscape.

Many of the smaller settlements simply disappeared, including Radbourne, Stoneton south of Priors Hardwick and Wormleighton. Whilst the first two of these have disappeared completely, a modern Wormleighton does exist, thanks largely to the presence of its manor, which was owned originally by the Spencer family, from whom Princess Diana was descended. The Spencers owned much of the land in this area and steadily sold much of it in order to finance the building of their current seat at Althorp. Today only a fragment remains of the original structure of Wormleighton Manor, which remains a private farm-house, the modern village largely of Victorian construction.

> Wormleighton Manor was originally four times the size of the Spencer's home at Althorp, but over time stained glass and oak panelling from the house were transported to the family's Northants home, which gradually assumed precedence.

Tudor times were generally auspicious for the area as the produce of its various and fertile estates found markets to the north and south. Many of the larger manor houses and halls which remain today were built during this time, with other families joining the Spencers with interests in the area including the Dudleys, who took ownership of Ladbroke Manor. Robert Dudley was the son of the Earl of Leicester and a 'favourite' of Queen Elizabeth.

The next set of events to make a mark on the local area took place during the Civil War, during which time a number of locations in this section suddenly emerged from relative obscurity into the limelight. Indeed, this is a theme that will recur and intensify as the canal winds its way closer to Oxford.

Southam was the site of one of the first engagements in Civil War in 1642, but its infamy began the year before when the king passed through the town and the churchwardens refused to ring the bells to make him welcome. Furious with their behaviour, the king had the church doors locked until they agreed to pay a fine of 13s 4d. The story didn't end there, however, as the bell ringers continued their defiance by refused to ring the bells to wish him 'Godspeed' as he left, leading Charles to send his footmen to levy a further 5s fine.

The battle itself was more of a skirmish and followed when Parliamentary forces led by Lord Brooke were encouraged to leave the meal they had just settled down to when they heard that a Cavalier force led by the Earl of Northampton was approaching. Brooke ordered an attack, which resulted in a handful of deaths.

Southam's position meant it became a favourite spot for gathering armies. King Charles himself slept at the Manor House on Market Hill two months after the battle and Cromwell was also a visitor, along with 7,000 troops, in 1645. The Civil War was also to prove the final nail in the coffin for

> The Manor House in Southam is now a chemist's shop and one of the most distinctive buildings in the town centre.

Wormleighton Manor. Used as a garrison by the king, it suffered a major fire during this time.

In some cases change in the local landscape occurred almost over-night; in others the movement was more gradual. Fenny Compton was not enclosed until 1769 and the land that had belonged to the Turchil family passed to the Holbechs of Farnborough, although the largest house in the village was owned by the Wyllys family. Unfortunately, however, the attractions of southern Warwickshire could not compete with the New World, and the family emigrated to America where its head became the first Governor of Connecticut. By 1764 the house had fallen into decay.

The Enclosure Act of 1761 had a significant impact upon land ownership in this and most rural areas. Land not already enclosed was consolidated into existing large farms. Shortly afterwards changes in transport infrastructure began a gradual thawing in the isolation of the local villages as roads were upgraded and turnpikes introduced. This was good news for places like Southam, favoured as it was by being at the junction of the Coventry–Banbury Road with the Welsh Drovers Road. The town rapidly became a coaching centre, which proved to be something of a respite for Southam, which had suffered from a devastating fire in 1741 destroying over thirty houses.

For many in the surrounding villages life probably went on much as it had before. Coaches rattling by on their way to Coventry, Oxford or even London would have had little relevance to their lives. The transport innovation that was to have an impact was the canal. Cutting through the heart of the previously quiet countryside, the very act of building the canal would have been a significant intrusion, and when the 'navvies' left, the local population found themselves with a direct route to towns that had previously existed only as exotic faraway locations.

Before long, the entrepreneurial instinct took hold and not only did farmers use the canal to find new markets but fresh industries also grew up, such as brick making at Napton. The canal's influence lingered as its great rival, the railway, failed to make a significant presence. Even Southam failed to link into the railway network, with local landowners often blocking progress. Equally, a proposed canal linking Lapworth with Priors Hardwick via Southam also came to nothing.

During the twentieth century the character of the local villages changed once more, and many were to a large extent rescued by the car as they found a new lease of life as desirable commuter villages. This was not at the cost of traditional farming, however, with most of the villages featured in this section retaining a strong farming presence, with farms at times located in the heart of the village itself.

More modern commercial activity is confined mainly to Southam and Fenny Compton, although the odd office can be found in converted farm buildings. In places such as Priors Hardwick it is the pub or restaurant that now pulls people into these villages, although without exception all reward a visit in their own right, and each seems to have developed its own sense of community rooted in the traditions and history that had so long to embed themselves before the outside world finally managed to intrude.

THE NATURAL LANDSCAPE

If anyone should tell you that ours is a crowded island, just bring them to this part of England and show them the view. This is an area of scattered villages, often hidden from each other, linked by vast tracts of farmland. Sandwiched between the southern Midlands and the northern Home Counties, this is a peaceful and picturesque part of Middle England.

It is also an area of contrasts, with hills to the north and east and flatlands to the west. The hills are formed of marlstone ironstone, a rock with a gingerish colour with occasional blue streaks of non-oxidised iron. This, along with local grey limestone, is evident mainly as building material, giving the villages hereabouts a distinctive but not unattractive dark-brown hue. To the north and west, blue lias, a clay-like limestone, predominates. With its combination of carbonate, silica, alumina and iron this material is perfect for cement manufacture and Southam was once a centre for this material.

A unusual wooden footbridge near Wormleighton.

As its name suggests, Napton on the Hill is perched on top of a dramatic rise, although its height of 45m above the canal appears more dramatic due to its steepness. Marston Hill to the south has a further 40m on Napton, but rises more gradually, whilst inclines to the south of Priors Hardwick though not quite so high are also impressive. As such, this stretch is blessed with a number of good viewpoints.

Woodland is noticeable by its absence with only the odd scattered spinney or fox covert. Natural water is equally scarce with the notable exception of a number of minor streams and the River Stowe flowing through Southam. Otherwise, it is man's influence bringing water to the area, both by the canal and through two significant reservoirs, Boddington in the south and Napton just off the map to the north, with the former a significant supplier of water to the canal.

ACCESS AND TRANSPORT

ROADS
This section is described to the north by the A425 linking Daventry and Leamington Spa and to the west by the A423 linking Coventry and Banbury. In between there is a network of minor roads, although these lie mainly to the east of the canal itself. Two of these roads cross east–west, one linking Fenny Compton with Upper Boddington and the other Priors Marston and Southam. A third road heads north from the

first of these and links up with the Priors Hardwick and Marston. The nearest motorway access is Junction 12 of the M40 where the B4451 heads northeast towards Southam, a total of approximately 4 miles.

RAIL

Unusually for this canal, the railway is absent on this stretch. The nearest station is Leamington Spa, 6 miles to the west of Southam. Otherwise, National Train Enquiries can be reached on 08457 484950.

BUSES

As reflects the largely rural nature of this area, bus services can be idiosyncratic and it is best to check the current status of services and timetables using the website provided by Warwickshire Council (see Learn More and Links).

Alternatively, Traveline (www.traveline.org.uk) on 0870 6082608 can give details of specific services between 7 a.m. and 10 p.m.

The most significant services in the area are run by the following companies:

- Johnsons of Henley (01564 797070).
  The Southam Shuttle, *a circular service taking in Napton, Priors Marston and Priors Hardwick from Monday-Saturday with five services a day.*
  The 277 linking Fenny Compton with Leamington Monday-Saturday with two services a day.
- The A&M Group (0500 212225).
  The Flexibus 214 *linking Priors Hardwick, Priors Marston and Napton to Rugby, with one service on Thursdays.*
  The Flexibus 497 *linking Ladbroke with Warwick and Leamington with one service on Tuesdays.*

  The Flexibus 499 *linking Ladbroke and Fenny Compton with Banbury with one service on Thursdays and Saturdays.*
  The Flexibus 500 *linking Napton and Southam with one service on Mondays and Fridays.*
- Stagecoach Midland Red (01788 535555).
  The 63 linking Southam to Rugby and Leamington Spa Monday-Saturday with an hourly service.
- Catteralls Coaches (01926 813840).
  The 503 linking Southam and Banbury, taking in Napton and Fenny Compton with one service on Thursdays and Saturdays.

TAXIS

Taxis firms in this section are mainly based in Southam and include:
- Cardells Private Hire (01926 812145).
- Executive Cars (01926 817878).
- Marshalls Cars (01926 812711).
- Specs Cars (01926 812711).

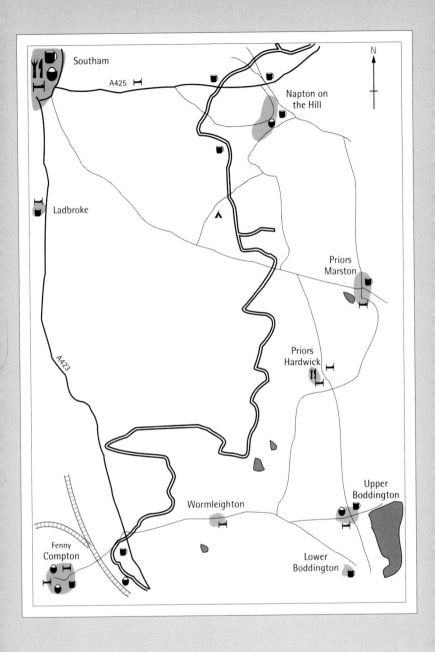

N

Southam

A425

Napton on
the Hill

Ladbroke

Priors
Marston

A423

Priors
Hardwick

Upper
Boddington

Wormleighton

Fenny
Compton

Lower
Boddington

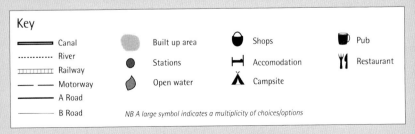

Key

━━━ Canal	▨ Built up area	◕ Shops
·········· River	● Stations	H Accomodation
▦▦▦ Railway	◗ Open water	⛺ Campsite
─ ─ Motorway		
━ A Road		☕ Pub
─ B Road	*NB A large symbol indicates a multiplicity of choices/options*	¶¶ Restaurant

BASICS

INTRODUCTION

If window shopping is your thing, you're in for a lean time when passing through this section. However, if your needs are more basic, or if you're interested in local produce, then with a little research you will get what you want. The relative independence of the local villages also means that they have tended to evolve according to their own needs and whims. This is a section with a number of one-pub or one-shop villages, but no two are the same so dip in and enjoy!

SHOPPING

Without question Southam is the main shopping centre along this section for basic supplies. In the High Street itself there is a Co-Op Late Store and an Acorn Stores convenience store as well as a Post Office and a pharmacy. There's also a selection of more specialist stores as well as a range of banks. Further down Market Hill on Oxford Street there is a Budgen's supermarket.

The town also still has a small town market every Tuesday selling everything from fruit and vegetables and meat through to clothing. The market takes place just off the High Street behind the Post Office, where there is also that rarity – a free public car park with clean public toilets. There is a farmers' market on the second Saturday of every month. Just outside Southam on the Welsh Road, a side route to Napton, there is also a garden centre.

Napton's shop (01926 812488) has recently undergone renovation and offers a wide range of services including an ATM, off-licence and food, as well as an in-store bakery. Basic chandlery and boat supplies are also available at the marina.

Goods available at the small village shop in Upper Boddington (01327 260245) range from emergency supplies and pet food through to freshly baked bread and coffee beans, all squeezed round a small Post Office counter. The shop also acts as an agent for various services such as dry cleaning.

Fenny Compton has a Co-Op late shop with an ATM. There is a hairdressing salon above it called, appropriately enough, A Cut Above (01295 770359). The marina (01295 770461) also offers basic boat supplies, but no food other than chocolate and ice cream – although sometimes that can be enough!

EATING AND DRINKING

Those looking for a bite to eat in this section are best directed to start with one of the village pubs. The food offered in these varies from solid pub grub through to high-class restaurant food, so it's best to do your research first if all you're after is a pie and a pint. In addition there are also a smattering of hotels and restaurants offering more formal dining.

> For many years Southam was known as a cider centre. In 1820 playbills at London's Drury Lane advertised only two drinks – Whitbread Ales and Southam Cider.

Otherwise Southam offers a range of cafés and takeaways if you really don't fancy a pub or restaurant, all in the High Street or Market Hill. These include the Courtyard Café (01926 815134), a sports bar offering English breakfasts and basic jacket potatoes as well as a range of teas, and Efes Takeway (01926 812568), which specialises in pizza. If it's fish and chips you want, try the Seastar (01926 814458).

Also in Southam there are four ethnic restaurants/takeaways. The Balti Hut (01926 815948) and Mumbai Blues (with its startlingly blue interior (01926 817847) both offer Indian food, whilst the Southam Kitchen (01926 810168) and China Hall (01926 812256) both serve Chinese food.

Southam's past as a coaching centre has left a legacy of pubs. Although there are nothing like the number there once was, there are still a few to choose from, including the low roofed eighteenth-century coaching inn the Bowling Green (01926 812575) and the Olde Mint (01926 812339), both on the High Street, as well as The Black Dog on

The Black Dog, Southam.

Market Hill (01926 813175). Also within Southam behind the High Street is the Bull Inn on, appropriately enough, Bull Street (01926 812505) and the Crown Inn just a little further down (01926 810622).

> The Black Dog is named after Piers Gaveston. A close friend and confidant of Edward II, although in the end this was to prove his comeuppance. Shortly after coming to the throne the king made his friend the earl of Cornwall, an act which was not taken kindly by the powerful earls of Warwick and Lancaster who had him kidnapped and subsequently executed in 1312.

On the hill within Napton is the Crown (01926 812484), which fits perfectly into the role of village centre pub with its skittle table, while down the hill towards the north, on the junction with the A425 is the Kings Head (01926 812202), which was saved from demolition by its brewery and is now a lively pub with two bars.

Actually on the canal there's the Bridge at Napton (01926 812466) where the A425 crosses the canal, a popular pub and restaurant, and the Folly (01926 815185), down the track from the Priors Marston road but well signposted. This was once a farmhouse and the tradition lives on in its excellent selection of pies, ranging from steak and kidney through lamb and apricot to chicken tikka.

> The Olde Mint (originally the Horse and Jockey) was renamed in recognition of the belief that it was used by Charles I to cast silver coins after the Battle of Edge Hill.

The Bell Inn at Ladbroke (01926 813562) has a large car park and is conveniently tucked away in the heart of the village, just off the A423. The pub can trace itself back to the eighteenth century and is the last of the three coaching inns that the village once boasted.

The Hollybush Inn at Priors Marston (01327 260934) has recently moved away from being an expensive restaurant towards re-discovering its village pub roots, but still serves more formal food on Thursday through to Saturday and bar meals on other days.

Although it may look like a pub, the Butchers Arms restaurant in Priors Hardwick (01327 260504) is worth a special mention. The building itself dates back to 1375 and its bar has an inglenook fireplace

> The sign for the Butchers Arms shows the Union Flag entwined with that of Portugal and points out the fact that Portugal is this country's oldest ally.

and flagstone floors, which betray its origins as a simple village pub. The food has a Portuguese theme and the restaurant has a number of private alcoves. There is even a cannonball, found during restoration work in the 1970s and said to date from the Battle of Edge Hill.

The recently re-thatched Plough in Upper Boddington (01327 260364) has a picture-postcard charm and has served as the village local since the sixteenth century. A Grade II Listed building, it was completely destroyed by fire in March 2003 and lovingly restored so that it was able to re-open just over a year later.

An extravagant painted 'Welcome' sign over the entrance to the Merrie Lion pub in Fenny Compton (01295 770881) makes the visitor feel exactly that. The Wharf Inn outside Fenny Compton (01295 770332) is actually on the canal and has recently been renovated to give a light modern feel and restaurant-style dining. The pub also has a comprehensive set of children's play equipment in the garden.

SLEEPING

Given this section's rural nature, it isn't surprising perhaps that a number of the local farms have turned their hand to catering for the visitor. Other large and often rather magnificent houses have also found this a useful way to supplement income and it is worth looking around to see if you can unearth a gem. There are also a couple of hotels with the usual facilities near Southam and a campsite outside Napton, which can be reached via a track from the canal.

HOTELS
The two hotels are:

- **The Stoneythorpe Hotel**, Southam (Warwick Road) 01926 812365 on the Warwick Road – *twenty-three bedrooms*.

- **The Tarsus Hotel**, Southam, Daventry Road (Daventry Road 01926 813585) – *a Greek and Turkish restaurant with twelve hotel rooms*.

BED AND BREAKFAST/GUESTHOUSES
The following is a selection of establishments offering bed and breakfast in this section:

- **Briarwood**, Warwick Road, Southam (01926 814756).
- **The Old Bakery**, Southam (01926 813225).
- **Hill Farm**, Priors Hardwick (01327 260338) – *farm-based rooms, capable of sleeping seven*.
- **Wormleighton Hall** (01295 770234) – *country-style accommodation set in farmland*.
- **Hollow Meadow House**, Priors Hardwick (01327 261540).

- **Hill Farm**, Priors Hardwick (01327 260338).
- **Marston House**, Priors Marston (01327 260297).
- **The Grange**, Fenny Compton (01295 770590).
- **Willow Cottage**, Fenny Compton (01295 770429).
- **High Acres Farm**, Upper Boddington (01295 750217) – *two bedrooms in a farmhouse overlooking the Cherwell Valley*.

CAMPING
Camping is possible at **NG Adkins Camp Site**, Holt Farm (01926 812225).

The canal just as it approaches Napton.

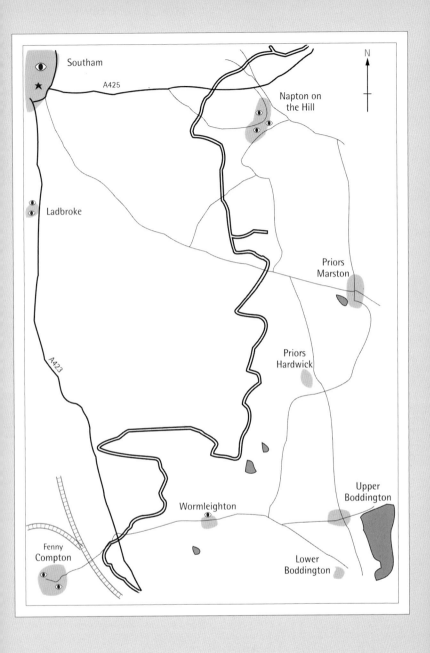

Southam

A425

Napton on
the Hill

Ladbroke

Priors
Marston

Priors
Hardwick

A423

Upper
Boddington

Wormleighton

Fenny
Compton

Lower
Boddington

N

Key

════ Canal		Built up area	◉	Site/Sight
·········· River	●	Stations	⊘	Leisure
▥▥▥ Railway				
─ ─ Motorway	◗	Open water	★	Entertainment
── A Road				
── B Road			🏰	Culture

NB A large symbol indicates a multiplicity of choices/options

SEEING AND DOING

INTRODUCTION

Southam, and to some extent Napton, in the north and Fenny Compton to the south of this section provide the main focal points for formal places to visit. It would be a mistake, however, to assume that the smaller villages have nothing to offer. Just because these lack a headline 'attraction' doesn't mean you can afford to pass them by, but rather should approach them with different expectations.

SIGHTS

Given its ancient position as the market town, and therefore main focus for activity in the north of the section, it's hardly surprising that Southam offers the most sights of interest to the casual visitor. Having gained its charter as early as the thirteenth century, and given its position on the east–west drovers road as well as the road linking Welsh markets to the Midlands, Southam has enjoyed a long history, many remnants of which remain today.

Of particular interest is the 'Halliwell', now know as the Holywell, the water from which was said to cure eye ailments. Water from this and other wells continued to supply the town until the mains came in the 1920s. In fact Southam has something of a pedigree in matters medical, having played host to the first free Provident Dispensary, established in 1818 by local surgeon Henry Lilley-Smith, who also founded an Eye and Ear Infirmary in what is now the Stoneythorpe Hotel.

As might be expected, given that Southam was once owned by Coventry Priory, the town's main church, St James', also has a long history, having been founded in 1294. It is notable both for its windows, which cover a range of styles, and its carvings, which include four green men.

> On the edge of Southam is Dallas Burston Polo Ground, the home of the Royal Leamington Spa Polo Club.

The chemist's shop in Southam's High Street was once the Manor House where King Charles I rested shortly after the Battle of Edge Hill, along with his son the prince of Wales and James, the Duke of York. With them as their tutor was

> Both the old Manor House and the Olde Mint are reputed to be haunted, the latter by a lady in a long white dress with lace hanging over her hands.

Dr William Harvey, later to become famous as the man who discovered the circulation of blood. The Olde Mint pub, an imposing stone edifice dating back to the fourteenth century, was where Charles I is thought to have minted coins for his troops after the Battle of Edgehill in 1642.

SECTION A

Napton of course is dominated by its iconic windmill, which lords itself over the village from the hill. This dates back to 1543, although the current structure was built around 1835, with some of the buildings surrounding it added in 1910. The mill has good stone foundations and is made of tarred red brick. Although it is not possible to visit the mill, a footpath goes all the way up to the entrance to the house before passing to the right.

> There were originally two Napton windmills. The current survivor lost two sails in a gale in 1976.

> Copies of a Napton Nature Trail leaflet, which takes you up to the reservoir and back, are available from inside the church.

This is worth doing for two reasons. First, the view just after the house is a good one, allowing the visitor to pick out the course of the canal. The second reason is the double-backed seat hidden away on the right on the road going up to the windmill. This was established on the 50th anniversary of the Blitz alongside a Rowan tree and marks the site of a look-out post from which the bombing of Coventry was witnessed by a team of powerless observers.

> The unusual chapel opposite the shop in Napton belongs to the Christadelphians, a group who believe the literal word of the Bible, that is to say they believe it to be error free and not open to interpretation. The list of service times has the caveat 'God Willing'.

Where the road bends you can cut through some trees to St Lawrence's church. The church has painted copies of records of donations to the poor dating back to 1816, including £50 left for equal division between twenty poor widows on St Thomas' Day in 1844 by a

Napton's Christadelphians church.

Mr Henry Bates. On reaching the canal, venture over to the Folly Inn which has a good collection of old farming equipment.

Ladbroke is picturesque and worth a visit, but it is a compact village and soon covered. Since being bypassed in 1985 it seems to have slipped into a dignified cocoon. A useful village trail on a notice board outside The Bell gives some pointers. Of particular interest are the mix of thatched and tiled buildings and the partial use of half-timbering. The village hall is something of an oddity, a wooden construct that originally saw service with the army during the First World War.

Talking of war, Ladbroke's small community was shaken up by the arrival of a Prisoner of War camp in Radbourne Lane now on the other side of the A423. Initially established for Italian prisoners, the regime was pretty relaxed, with one prisoner being allowed to collect pails of water from a local farm and the whole troop marching every Sunday to the Convent in Southam for Mass. As they marched, they wore a plain brown uniform with a large red cross on their back to give a target should they try to escape.

In time the camp became a holding station for German prisoners of war and high security fences were installed, with locals advised to steer clear. The camp continued after the war, becoming a centre for people displaced from Estonia and Latvia, when it gained its current name of 'The Polish Camp'. There are still a couple of old huts there, evoking an image of what the place must once have been like.

Ladbroke also has a Millennium Green with a playground, a wild flower meadow, and a Millennium Stone (complete with buried time capsule) as well as four oaks.

Priors Hardwick and Priors Marston are also pretty to visit, but have nothing like the range of actual sights. Together with Wormleighton

Priors Hardwick War Memorial and Lychgate.

they form a single parish with a population of only around 1,000. Both churches date back to the thirteenth century and each is worth visiting.

It is Wormleighton, the smallest of the three that perhaps holds the most interest. If you descend the lane just before St Peter's church towards the end of the village and cross over the stile you will find yourself in a field which today is grazed by sheep but was once the medieval centre of the village. The various bumps on the surface provide a thin veneer to centuries of history and give an idea of how big the village would once have been. Back in the heart of the modern (mainly Victorian) village you can see the Spencer Gatehouse leading into the heart of the Manor and St Peter's itself is worth a visit for its Perpendicular screen.

It can take a while to orientate yourself in Fenny Compton as it seems to have a number of candidates for its centre, none of which are assertive enough to give the village a heart. The church of St Peter and St Paul is a classic example of local stone whilst near the entrance to the church is the tiny old school house. The best thing to do here is probably simply wander and see what takes your fancy, be it the sundials, the wooden Warwickshire Bear cum signpost or the church, with its wayward tower and eighteenth-century rectory.

Just to the west of Fenny Compton is Burton Dassett Hills Country Park, which was opened in 1971 and has proved popular ever since. One of the site's greatest features is as a spectacular viewpoint from which it is possible to look out onto great swathes of Warwickshire including the canal. Quite understandably there was also once a windmill here too, the remains of which still stand. The site itself is a series of irregular hillocks grazed by sheep, and has a number of picnic spots scattered over its 100 acres, although there is a charge to park your car. Information on the surrounding area, including cycleways, is also available here.

CULTURE AND ENTERTAINMENT

Sandwiched between the cultural centres of Warwick and Leamington Spa to the north and Banbury to the south, and given the fact that most of the villages in this section are very small, it is hardly surprising that culture and entertainment are thin on the ground along this section. That said, Southam Club on School Road was set up to provide a community focus for traditional games and runs regular darts, pool and dominoes nights as well as other more ad hoc entertainment (01926 812284), and there's also a leisure centre with swimming pool (01926 817788).

Napton also plays host to an annual boat gathering, normally held over the third weekend in September at the Top Lock with a barbeque, music, auction and a quiz night. Some of the villages have their own sports clubs, and most (although not all) have childrens' playgrounds, although some can be hard to find.

Spencer Gate, Wormleighton.

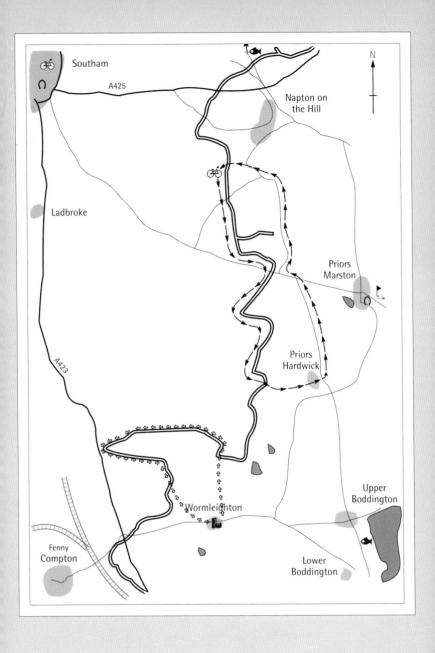

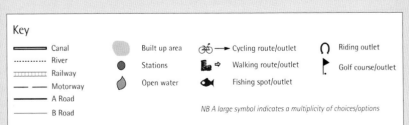

Key

━━━	Canal	Built up area	🚲➜	Cycling route/outlet	∩ Riding outlet
┈┈┈	River	Stations	🚶⇨	Walking route/outlet	Golf course/outlet
▥▥▥	Railway	Open water	🐟	Fishing spot/outlet	
╴ ╴ ╴	Motorway				
━━━	A Road				
──	B Road				

NB A large symbol indicates a multiplicity of choices/options

SAMPLING

INTRODUCTION

The rise of the Napton Flight of locks brings the canal to its summit, which in turn means that the canal's engineers were keen to preserve a good length between this and the next set of locks at Claydon to act as a giant reservoir feeding the canal either side. This is supplemented by the large Boddington Reservoir to the east and the Clattercote Reservoir encountered in the next section, both offering good walking and fishing opportunities.

Access to the canal is sporadic but possible, with the large Warwickshire flatlands to the northwest of the section largely bereft of either population or transport links, barring one minor road. What marks this section out is its collection of small pretty villages and its almost overwhelming peaceful rural nature, offering plenty of opportunities to explore.

The OS Explorer Maps covering this area are numbers 206, Edge Hill and Fenny Compton and 222 Rugby and Daventry.

WALKING

In addition to the towpath there are plenty of walking opportunities in this area, although there are no formal routes. Three footpaths head north out of Fenny Compton and there is a network of paths linking the villages of Upper Boddington, Priors Hardwick and Priors Marston which criss-cross the fields and tackle the at-times steep ridges to the east of the canal.

Priors Marston acts in fact as something of a magnet for local footpaths, with no less than seven emanating from the village, including one that strikes out due east over Marston Hill giving good views of the surrounding country-side. Two more head north and link

The Oxford Canal walk is well signposted.

up before linking with a small road into Marston Doles, where the path continues northwards to join the approach into the south of Napton.

There are another set of paths to the south of Napton, with one heading west over the hill towards Southam, whilst another heads southwest before forking southeast on the Welsh Road towards Priors Hardwick.

A 4-mile Napton Nature Trail guide in and around Napton is also available from St Lawrence's church, the majority of which takes place north of the A425, taking in Napton Reservoir and a stretch of both the Grand Union and South Oxford canals.

Walk A begins outside the church in Wormleighton, 2 miles to the east of Fenny Compton, and has been designed to incorporate the wide extravagant sweep that is perhaps one of the most distinguishing features of the South Oxford Canal.

> The extravagance of this bend may seem to take the art of contour hugging to an extreme level. The truth, however, is that the canal's engineers were refused permission to build locks here by the owners of Wormleighton Manor. In their view a lock would have given too good an opportunity for boatmen to pause and poach something tasty for their dinner!

SECTION A WALK

From Wormleighton and Back

Description:	*An easy stroll along a generally good foot-path with a slight hill either side.*
Distance:	*4 miles*
Duration:	*1.5hrs*
Starting point:	*Grid Reference 448538, OS Explorer 206*
Nearest Refreshment:	*The Wharf Inn on the A423 towards Fenny Compton.*

Park in the lay-by on the right, on the road leading down to the church. Start by heading north past the manor and the church using the road which turns into a track heading downhill through a field by a barn. Continue straight ahead and through the next field also, at the end of which you will come across Bridge 128. Cross over and pick up the towpath heading left, in a westerly direction.

Follow the towpath round its wide sweep, taking the opportunity to absorb the view to the right (north) when it appears. The water executes a sharp curve at Wormleighton Grange where there is also an interesting footbridge. Leave the towpath at Bridge 133 and of the two footpaths you are offered take the one heading right, in a south-easterly direction.

The path now takes you over a large expanse of uneven grass and you are in fact walking across the ruins of the medieval village of Wormleighton. On reaching a metal gate cross the stile and head up the concrete road which brings you back to the church where you turn right and head back to your starting point.

CYCLING

Cycling is best confined to the northern reaches of this section where the towpath linking the Napton Flight and Marston Doles locks is on the whole solid, although care should be taken when using it as these same characteristics make it attractive to walkers and boat crew working the locks. In the less busy southern stretch the path can get very bumpy.

The canal is easily accessible at both Napton and Fenny Compton, and there are two further crossing points at Marston Doles and off the road leading past Napton Holt camp site, as well as a number of smaller tracks, notably one at Priors Hardwick. Three roads cross the canal to the north of Napton, including that at Napton Bridge Inn (Bridge Number 111), and there is also a useful little track leading down to the Folly Pie pub at the top of the locks where there is convenient parking. The towpath can be rocky north of this point so this is a better point to start a ride.

Access at Fenny Compton is best achieved where the busy A423 crosses over the waterway, again near a pub, this time the Wharf Inn, where there is roadside parking. It is possible to cycle north of this point, and those seeking solitude may even prefer it, although the brambles can be a problem in parts.

Our suggested route starts at Folly Bridge (Number 113) and heads south along the towpath following the path of the locks all the way to Bridge 124, a distance of just over 4 miles, before picking up the track on the left into Priors Hardwick. Once in the village turn left and left again past the church and on reaching the T-junction again turn left, heading north towards Marston Doles.

Turn left at the next T-junction on the Marston Doles to Priors Marston road and then take the first right just before the canal. Follow this for 1.5 miles until you reach a junction where you continue straight ahead and into Napton. Turn left at Holroyd Farm and back to your starting point – a total of around 13 miles.

Bike shops along the route include Rockingham's Cycle Store, Southam (01926 812685).

RIDING

This section is not particularly well-endowed with public bridleways, although the local roads tend to be fairly quiet and suitable for a steady ride. There are two main stretches worthy of mention; a 4-mile run of bridleway linking Wormleighton with Marston Doles, following a flattish course to the west of the canal with a side spur leading into Priors Hardwick. This route can be extended a mile further to the west taking the rider past Wormleighton Grange but this just brings you out onto the A423.

There are also a few short runs to the south and east of Priors Hardwick linking up with local roads from which it is possible to stitch a ride together. The other main public bridleway heads north out of Priors Marston and up into Napton, passing through the village and downhill onto the busy A425. Not surprisingly, riding supplies and services tend to be thin on the ground in these parts.

Riding Establishments along this stretch include:

- **Broadwell Cross Country Course,** Broadwell on the A426 out of Southam (01926 812347).
- **Chestnut Farm Livery,** Priors Marston (01327 260759).
- **A&J Saddlery and Clothing** (01926 812238).

FISHING

Those looking for canal fishing along this stretch should contact:

- **Leamington Liberal AC** – *Folly Bridge to Napton Junction.*
- **Cowroast Marina AC** (01295 770461) – *Fenny Compton Marina to Bridge 136.*

As well as from the canal, fishing is available at two reservoirs, one in the area covered by the map and one just out of it to the north:

- **Boddington Reservoir** (01295 270796) – *a 65-acre lake stocked mainly with good tench up to 5lb, perch to 12oz and roach up to a pound as well as good-sized pike. The lake is also a nature reserve however, so beware of the native birdlife.*
- **High Clays Farm,** Southam (01926 814557) – *mainly carp and roach.*
- **Napton Reservoir** (Just north of Napton near Calcutt Marina on the Grand Union Canal (01203 612880) – *originally two lakes but now merged into one, which has dispersed the fish a little. This lake has a reputation for big fish, including carp, tench of 6lb plus and roach, as well as bream of up to 10lb.*

Fishing supplies are best obtained in either Leamington Spa or Banbury.

OTHER

The nearest golf course is just to the east of the map at **Hellidon Lakes Country Club,** Hellidon (to the east of Priors Marston, 01327 262550) – 18 holes, 6642yds and 9 holes, 2791yds. Also includes a putting green, tuition, pro-shop and practice area.

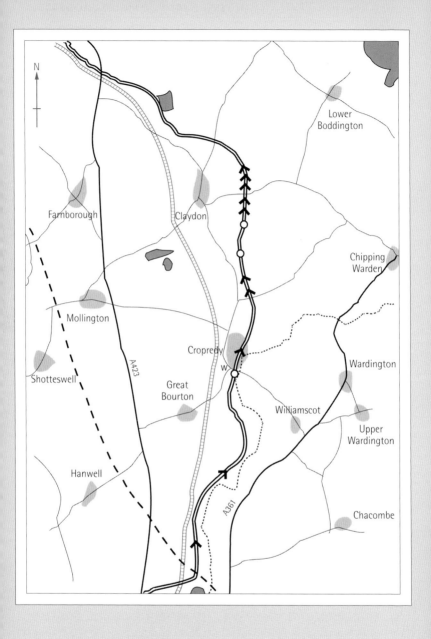

Key

━━━ Canal	⬤ Built up area
⋯⋯ River	⬤ Stations
▦▦ Railway	⬤ Open water
▬ ▬ Motorway	
━━ A Road	◯ Turning point
— B Road	⚓ Lock
	Ⓑ Boatyard
	W Waterpoint

SHAPERS

THE CANAL ON THIS STRETCH

KEY FACTS

LENGTH: 8 miles

BOATYARDS: 0
Clattercote Wharf is run as a private mooring.

WATERPOINTS: 1
   Cropredy

TURNING POINTS: 3
   Clattercote Wharf
   North of Elkington's Bridge
   Cropredy Wharf

LOCKS: 11
   Claydon Flight – 5 locks (30ft 6in)
   Elkington's Lock (6ft 5in)
   Varney's Lock (5ft 10in)
   Broadmoor Lock (7ft 3in)
   Cropredy Lock (5ft 6in)
   Slat Mill Lock (8ft 0in)
   Bourton Lock (6ft 5in)

A delightfully quiet stretch interrupted by the welcome presence of Cropredy. The abandoned Fenny Compton Tunnel along with Claydon locks provide interest to the north, while the well-worn nature of the towpath south of Cropredy provides testament to the popularity of this stretch amongst walkers and cyclists alike.

Cross over the Marina bridge and pick up the towpath as it curves round and into the long straight of the Fenny Compton 'Tunnel'. The path here is firm and crosses over the canal at the metal Bridge 137 where there is also access to the A423 and a convenient parking spot. A sign announces that this bridge was rebuilt in Golden Jubilee year 2002.

This stretch has been much tidied in recent years. Boaters used to have to cross their fingers and hope nothing was coming the other way, with not only shallow edges to cope with but a great deal of overhanging foliage, which was also an encumbrance for walkers and cyclists. Even today passing can be tricky in places, and the deep cutting acts as a reminder of how this was once a tunnel.

After the 'tunnel' the towpath becomes less defined but remains mostly solid and the railway closes in briefly from the right. The canal passes through a disused and decapitated railway bridge and swings first left, then right. A high hedge obscures Wormleighton Reservoir on the left while to the right the view is a continuation of the flatlands seen in the previous section.

The first Oxford Canal lift bridge comes and goes, as does the feeder bridge from the reservoir, which straddles the towpath sideways on. After another wide curve, this time to the right, Claydon Locks begin, just before which there is a run of good mooring.

> Fenny Compton did originally have a tunnel and, at 1,138yds, an impressive one at that. Although it had passing places it became a bottleneck and in 1838 the canal company bought all the land above the tunnel and promptly opened out the two ends and a bit in the middle. By 1870 even these two remaining underground stretches had gone.

These locks are nicely spread out, allowing those with responsibility for working them to enjoy a series of short walks between bouts of effort. At the middle lock from Bridge 145 there is a long straight track into Claydon and its museum. After the bottom lock the towpath loses some of its firmness, but is wide and easy going. A long straight stretch here makes for good mooring and concludes with a sharp 90-degree bend to the left followed swiftly by a bridge (Number 147). There's also a turning point here.

After the bridge the mooring remains reasonable and there is another bend, this time to the right, marking the beginning of a broad U-shaped curve after which there is another sweep to the right to reinstate the generally southerly direction. Along this stretch is Clattercote Wharf, a combination of private moorings, windmill and farm where, if you're lucky and depending on the time of year, you'll see a profusion of sunflowers or maybe pumpkins growing. Look out also for the eclectic scarecrows.

Elkington's Lock soon follows alongside Oathill Farm, where there is an old brick outhouse. The short stretch between here and Varney's Lock seems to be occupied by semi-permanent moorers, although a useful length of towpath is available for mooring (14-day maximum). There's also a slipway here on the non-towpath side that is available for private hire (07950 480032).

Just before Broadmoor Lock there is a collection of wooden hulled boats in various states of repair on the opposite bank, including one which, not to put too fine a point on it, has sunk. A fender maker offers mooring pins and windlasses and Sue Frances sells pots and plants, including herbs (01295 758438).

The long straight into Cropredy begins after Bridge 150 and the towpath immediately becomes more defined. The spire of the vil-

> Look out for the Bridge poem at Cropredy Lock.

lage's church is also pronounced on the horizon, acting as a beacon drawing you in. Some more long-term mooring follows, but if you

Fenny Compton Tunnel.

intend to moor in Cropredy, remain patient as there is a way to go yet and, given the village's popularity, mooring is not always guaranteed.

After BW's Cropredy North long-term moorings there's a stretch of 48-hour mooring before Cropredy Lock, where there's no short-age of signs advertising the vil-lage's main attractions, and after the locks a short run of visitors' mooring followed by a long stretch available on long-term permits. Cropredy is truly a canal village.

Bridge poem, Cropredy.

The moorings continue all the way to Cropredy Mill where there's a small spring amongst the trees.

The towpath between here and Banbury is impressively solid and worn, suggesting that this is a favourite route for walkers and cyclists alike. High hedges and trees hide the views to the left, but on the other side the familiar theme seen before Cropredy, of flat cultivated fields rising slowly onto a ridge, returns. This is a peaceful stretch, with the sense of solitude broken only by the railway.

The canal assumes a south-easterly direction for a while after Bridge 156 and the deep Slat Mill Lock. This ends with a kink in the water and a series of winding curves that tease the water to follow a more southerly course. Rare glimpses between the hedges reveal the level ground of the Cherwell Valley, soon to become a constant companion.

The well-kept Bourton Lock, the penultimate before Banbury, sits amongst grazing sheep and cattle in the meadow below. From here the banks may seem reassuringly solid but they can be deceptive, so take care. The source of the escalating hum from the right now becomes apparent as canal and motorway re-acquaint, after which a run of reinforced banks brings you to Hardwick Lock. Soon after this the railway takes its turn to cross the water and a long sweep round Banbury Reservoir provides a gentle introduction to the town itself.

PRINCIPAL TOWNS AND VILLAGES ON THIS STRETCH

CHACOMBE

Sitting on the Oxfordshire and Northamptonshire border, Chacombe dates back to the Bronze Age and was once defined by the bustle of its Priory. These days it is altogether more sleepy, the main excitement since King Charles I lined up his troops here before the Battle of Cropredy Bridge being the stray bombs which hit the village during the Second World War.

CHIPPING WARDEN

Chipping Warden's position on the Banbury to Coventry road meant it was once an important market town, but these days the busy road effectively cuts the village in two. The church of St Peter and St Paul and one of the village's pubs sit on one side of the divide with more modern housing, a large industrial estate and another pub on the other. The town was razed by a fire in the fifteenth century and never really recovered, but it is worth pausing to see the steps of the old medieval market outside the church.

> Chipping Warden's name is derived from the old English word 'ccopan', meaning 'to buy', suggesting that it has always relied on its market to survive, with Warden referring to the watch that was kept from Warden Hill.

CLAYDON

A typical farming village which retains its ironstone heart, but is dotted on its edges by more modern brick and rendered housing. The chequerboard brickwork on the farm outbuildings is worth seeing, as is the church of St James the Great and the Bygones Museum. The most northerly parish in Oxfordshire, the village stands on two road junctions, the western arm of which leads back to the A423. The southern road leads to Cropredy and that in the north to Boddington.

CROPREDY

Although today it can appear as if Cropredy owes its existence to the canal, its history in fact goes back much further and in 1644 the fields to its north were the site of a Civil War battle, named after the bridge over the Cherwell. The canal in fact acts as the eastern boundary to the village and as such canal users are well advised to wander off the towpath in order to experience the serendipities that Cropredy offers.

FARNBOROUGH

Farnborough probably owes its existence to the junction of the ancient tracks of Old Street and the Ridgeway, both of which pre-date Stonehenge, and latterly to the presence of the impressive Farnborough Hall. The village has a picturesque heart with its inn providing a perfect focal point. The area to the north of the village is dominated by Windmill Hill and its more modern housing, whilst the Hall and its lakes define the southern limit.

GREAT BOURTON

A deceptively spread out village clustered round its pub and the church of All Saints, with the latter notable for its unusual lychgate and bell tower. Sitting on a hill on the road linking the A423 with Cropredy, the buildings on one side of the main road, including the local village hall, sit on top of a slight embankment.

HANWELL

Another small ironstone village just north of Banbury, notable chiefly for its twelfth-century church hidden away down a private road as well as its (privately owned) castle.

LITTLE BOURTON

A mile to the south of Great Bourton, but easily accessed via The Plough on the A423, this village consists essentially of runs of houses off a circular one-way system.

LOWER BODDINGTON

A compact and pretty village with a range of building styles sitting on top of a hill from which there are some spectacular views. There are working farms in the centre and edge of the village as well as a pub.

MOLLINGTON

A pretty village perched on the edge of a hill with little to visit other than the church. The name is said to derive from 'molling', the process of making natural paints from the ores that bubbled up from local springs, with the Domesday Book confirming the village as being a place of wells and springs.

SHOTTESWELL

A village spread out over a hill with a warren of single-track roads and an unfocused centre. Recent building has, by and large, been sympathetic to the ironstone heritage. In between the houses there is the occasional good view looking eastwards, especially from the church.

UPPER WARDINGTON

A scattered village on a hill, with an impressive manor house in the centre hidden away behind railings. Unusually, the nearby Wesleyian chapel has a large rose window on one side. The village consists mainly of stone-built houses and seems to have resisted modern development.

WARDINGTON

Split between Lower Wardington on the A361 and Upper Wardington (see above), unusually for this stretch this is a village with two pubs. Wardington Manor, occupied appropriately by Lord Wardington, connects the two along with the imposing church of St Mary Magdalene.

> Wardington Manor was badly damaged by fire in April 2004. Nearly 100 firemen tackled the blaze and a similar number of villagers formed a human chain to salvage priceless possessions.

WILLIAMSCOT

It is difficult to imagine, but 200 years ago this small settlement just off the A361 on the road to Cropredy had three inns, a school and several shops. A hundred years later thirty-five buildings

> Charles I was said to have slept in 'a very poor man's house at Willamscot' after the Battle of Cropredy Bridge.

had been demolished and it became the hamlet it is today. Technically, Williamscot is part of Wardington to the north on the A361.

HISTORY

This section is encased in the northern tip of Oxfordshire and includes parts of Northamptonshire to the east and Warwickshire to the west. It is a predominately rural area around which are dotted a number of small villages, none of which dominates. Collectively these are often known as the Ironstone villages, from the local stone. After a while they can all begin to look the same, but don't be fooled as they each have their own identity which they guard jealously to this day.

Almost without exception the villages have their roots in Anglo Saxon times. Although there is evidence of much earlier settlement, such as the discovery of a Bronze Age flint in Chacombe, this does not seem to have been an area with a great deal of prehistoric life. Most can trace themselves back to the Domesday Book, and taking Chacombe as an example again this record indicates a settlement with twenty villagers, nine smallholders with eight ploughs and two slaves! Likewise nearby Cropredy is also mentioned and, like Chacombe, is recorded as being part of the estate held by the Bishop of Lincoln.

Each of the villages has its own church, of course, and many of these can also date themselves back to the twelfth and thirteenth centuries, suggesting that the communities within them would have been fairly settled by around that time. These churches have provided a centre of village life for over 900 years and continue today to act as a focal point for both religious and more secular life.

St Peter's church in Hanwell can trace itself back to 1154, with the oldest parts of the fabric dating back to around 100 years after that. The Norman font in this church has been used to baptise new Hanwell residents for nearly 800 years. Only recently has the church removed its solid wooden pews in favour of stackable chairs so that a space can more easily be cleared for concerts and other performances.

Like similar settlements across the country, the Ironstone villages survived through agriculture, with the feudal system supplying a local lord of the manor to oversee matters. Whilst often a local family, this was just as often a religious institution, with the Bishopric of Lincoln again a dominant player. A good example of this is Clattercote Priory which used to stand between Claydon and Cropredy, the remains of which are now a private residence. Originally a leper colony founded in the mid-twelfth century by Robert de Chesney, Bishop of Lincoln, this was converted to a priory of Gilbertine canons soon after 1246.

> On the site of the modern Calltercote Reservoir, pools once stood where the lepers of Clattercote St Leonard's Hospital bathed.

Farming required markets and Chipping Warden fulfilled this role. In the same way that the A361 now largely defines the village in the way that it cuts through it, it was another road, the ancient Welsh Road, that was instrumental in giving Chipping

> In a field near Chipping Warden the Battle of Danesmoor took place in 1649. A bloody battle between Lancastrians and Yorkists, the battle led to the destruction of many of the homes and crops in the area.

Norton a strategic location and, in turn, a role as the local market town. The old medieval market steps outside the church gave a good vantage point for the auctioneer.

A more modern reminder of the area's farming heritage is Claydon, where the Bygones Museum hosts a collection of nineteenth- and twentieth-century agricultural equipment. Between the medieval period and more modern farming there were the Enclosures. Like similar

SECTION B

SECTION A   NAPTON JUNCTION TO FENNY COMPTON

Above: *The remains of the old windmill on the windswept hill of Burton Dassett Park.*

Opposite above left: *Fenny Compton seems to have a profusion of sundials, of which this is one.*
Opposite above right: *The Folly pub in Napton is famous for its pies, and is keen to advertise itself.*
Opposite below: *It's easy to imagine what the POW Camp at Ladbroke would have been like 50 years ago.*

Ut umbra sic vita

THE MERRIE LION

THE
FOLLY
PIE PUB
1/4 MILE
Last pub
for 5 hours
CHILDREN WELCOME

communities across the country the Ironstone villages were about to have their order turned upside-down. Nowhere is this better illustrated than in Edgcote, half a mile southwest of Chipping Warden. In 1377 this community was recorded as having ninety-five people aged over four-teen, all paying the Poll Tax, indicating a substantial settlement, and it can be assumed that this total continued to grow over the following century. But in 1502 the local Chauncy family decided to enclose 240 acres of land in order to provide grazing for 500 sheep.

The effect was devastating, and over the succeeding decades the village steadily declined. Over this period the Chauncys were able to build a new home on the back of their profits from the sheep, one grand enough to provide shelter to King Charles on the eve of the Battle of Edgehill in 1642. A grand home needs a garden however, and in the early eighteenth century the family demolished what was left of the village in order to build a landscaped park running down to the Cherwell. Edgcote was effectively wiped off the map.

The fashion for gardens was not isolated to the Chauncys. Over in Farnborough the local hall was built by the Holbech family in the mid-eighteenth century, and the family remains in residence to this day. A key feature of the property is its gardens, which, like Edgcote, include some landscaped lakes.

Painful as they must have been, the Enclosures laid the foundation for a period of relative economic prosperity founded on sheep and more particularly wool. Local landowners, often including Oxford colleges, came together to gain the required Acts of Parliament for an enclosure, often on the pretext that the land was being woefully under-exploited. An old way of life, not universally successful but known and under-stood, passed by.

When the power of feudal lords and the local priories began to wane a new class of landowners with money and influence began to emerge. Fresh names came forward, includ-ing the Holbechs and the Copes in Hanwell. The most famous member of this family was probably Sir Anthony Cope, who was impris-oned in the Tower of London in 1587 for his Puritanical views.

If the enclosures were to be a defining moment for this area another was, undoubtedly, the Civil War. Scarcely a village in this section cannot claim to have a

> Hanwell was something of a centre of Puritanism. The Puritan preacher John Dod thrived under Sir Anthony Cope's patronage and gained the nickname the Decalogist after his tract based on the Ten Commandments. Some Cavalier soldiers captured him and put him in a tree, demanding a sermon on malt. Using his wit and experience he duly obliged and was released.

Civil War story, but the one with the best tale to tell is Cropredy. With the king having raised his standard in Oxford this area was largely Royalist, in practice if not in theory. Having operated from the univer-sity city for two years in 1644, he decided to send a large part of his army towards the Midlands in order to relieve the pressure on the troops

Clattercote Wharf.

led by his nephew Prince Rupert, as well as to reduce the burden on the city of billeting his troops.

Cromwell ordered his General Waller to follow, and he dutifully marched from Gloucester to Hanwell Castle, which was more fortified home than castle. What followed is probably more accurately described as a skirmish than a battle, but it was one of the opening conflicts of the war and as such deserves a place in the history books (see 'Seeing and Doing'). Four miles to the west of Mollington lies Edge Hill, site of an altogether more significant battle, the first major one of the Civil War in which 40,000 Royalists are said to have been slaughtered.

This section also sees the River Cherwell beginning to exert its presence, a geographical feature that has had a large part to play in the shaping of the area's history. The river rises at Hellidon, just east of Priors Marston in the previous section, but only becomes recognisable as a river at Edgcote, before passing under the A361 near Chipping Warden on the way to Cropredy.

From here the river's valley becomes the course followed by the canal for most of the rest of the journey to Oxford. The pastures created by the Cherwell's floodplain provide excellent grazing for sheep and cattle and helped to shape the area's period of prosperity in the seventeenth and eighteenth centuries.

The name of Cropredy keeps coming up, and one of its most distinguishing features is how it has adapted to the changes thrust upon it. Originally owned by the bishops of Lincoln, it fell to the Crown before it was sold by Elizabeth to the Boothby family, who in turn sold much of the surrounding land to Brasenose College around 200 years ago.

During the Enclosures many of its indigenous population were forced out of the cottages in the centre of the village towards more modest property on the outskirts. The empty farmhouses were subsequently converted by local tradespeople, with a particularly good example being the row of cottages which includes the Red Lion pub today.

Red Lion Street became home to tradesmen such as masons, tailors, saddlers and shoemakers. When the canal came in 1790 the village was well placed to take advantage of the opportunities it offered and

SECTION A   NAPTON JUNCTION TO FENNY COMPTON

Above: *Napton's locks are slow but steady.*

Opposite: *Boats queuing to start the Napton Flight at the Bottom Lock.*

it wasn't long before Cropredy became a thriving canal centre. The modern-day British Waterways depot used to be a coal wharf and the canal company established a toll office here. There was also a brick-works in the village which provided work for both local men and those in a number of surrounding villages. The canal also changed the local landscape, leading to the creation of two reservoirs.

Today Cropredy continues to trade successfully on its canal past and the length of canal going through it is one long line of permanent and temporary moorings. As if to prove the village's credentials as a survi-vor, the canal has thrived whilst the Great Western Railway which once stopped in the village now passes through scarcely noticed, and the old station, tucked away to the west of the village, has long since gone.

THE NATURAL LANDSCAPE

Given the proximity of this section to the canal's summit, it should come as no surprise that it plays host to large expanses of water. Wormleighton Reservoir sits right beside the canal, whilst Clattercote Reservoir lies just off one of the roads linking Claydon with the busy A423 and Boddington Reservoir nestles in the top north-eastern corner of the stretch.

Both these are owned by British Waterways and offer good fishing, with the water from Boddington flowing into the canal sideways-on at Bridge 142. There's another generous expanse of water to the west, although this, known as Sourland Pool, is an integral part of the grounds of Farnborough Hall.

The River Cherwell also makes its first appearance along this stretch, winding in from the east and picking up some momentum from springs south of Chipping Warden. From this point on the Cherwell provides a faithful companion to the canal for much of the route from here to Oxford. The water theme is continued with a myriad of other small streams and rivulets, the most significant of which is the Highfurlong Brook which starts at Boddington and flows parallel to the canal from east of Claydon Locks to Cropredy, where it finally surrenders to the Cherwell.

During its early stages, the landscape along this stretch is hidden behind the trees lining the sides of the defunct Fenny Compton Tunnel. These give way after a mile, but high hedges on the towpath side con-tinue to obscure the view to the east, which is in fact largely flat and featureless. Hills rise to the west, up top of which sit Farnborough, Mollington and Bourton. After Cropredy, the Cherwell Valley takes over on the towpath side, the east, and there are a number of wide meadows where geese and ducks like to linger.

A feature worth looking out for is the clear evidence of ridge and furrow farming, particularly around Elkington's and Varney's locks. The area's rural heritage is also apparent in its hedgerows, which, to the north at least, are made up of hawthorn and Midland thorn. Further evidence of ancient hedges can also be seen in the occasional hazel dogwood and field maple.

The land rises fairly steeply to the west and less so to the east, with the canal sitting in a natural valley accentuated by the presence of the Cherwell towards the south. Drawn by the same advantages, the railway sweeps in from the northwest and shares the narrow gap into Banbury with the canal and the Cherwell.

ACCESS AND TRANSPORT

ROADS
Most of this stretch sits in the 'V' formed by the A423 heading northeast and the A361 heading northwest out of Banbury. The two are linked by a web of roads within which Cropredy, Great Bourton and Claydon all sit in relative isolation. Farnbourgh and Mollington sit just to the west of the A423, whilst Shooteswell and Hanwell lie a little deeper off this road. Chipping Warden and Wardington sit on the A361, whilst Williamscot lies just off it on the way to Cropredy.

RAIL
Although the railway is a close companion of the canal along this stretch there are no stops. The nearest access by rail is Banbury. Otherwise, National Train Enquiries can be reached on 08457 484950.

BUSES
The villages in this section are linked by a variety of local bus routes, the most significant of which are:

- The 510, run by **Cheney Coaches** (01295 254254), *which links Farnborough, Mollington, Claydon, Cropredy and the Bourtons to Banbury with four buses a day Monday-Saturday.*
- The 4, run by **Geoff Amos Coaches** (01327 246461), *which links Wormleighton and Banbury via Claydon and Cropredy on Thursdays.*
- The 54, run by **Cherwell Villager** (01295 273086), *which links Mollington, Cropredy and Banbury on Tuesdays.*

Bus routes and times are subject to change, however, and it is advisable to check before relying on a particular service. A comprehensive summary of current services is available on the Oxfordshire County Council website (see Learn More and Links). Alternatively, Traveline (www.traveline.org.uk) on 0870 6082608 can give details of specific services between 7 a.m. and 10 p.m.

TAXIS
Taxi companies serving this area include **Silver Service**, Chipping Warden (01295 660565).

SECTION B

SECTION A   NAPTON JUNCTION TO FENNY COMPTON

Above: *Napton 's wndmill is privately owned, but a footpath goes right up to it.*

Opposite above: *Southam church sits proudly on the hill in that town.*
Opposite below: *The public tap in Priors Hardwick acts as a reminder of times before 'mod cons'.*

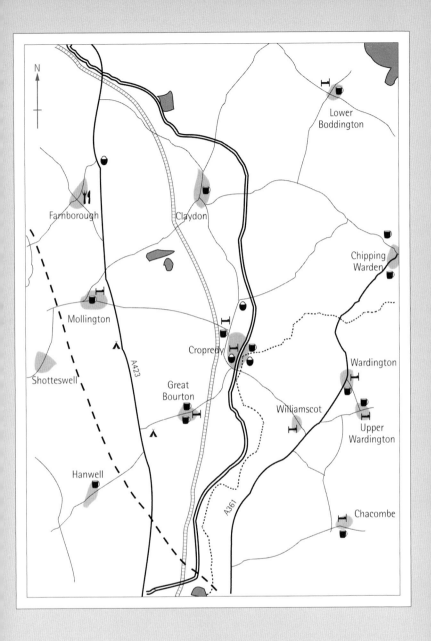

N

Lower
Boddington

Farnborough

Claydon

Chipping
Warden

Mollington

Cropredy

Wardington

Shotteswell

A423

Great
Bourton

Williamscot

Upper
Wardington

Hanwell

A361

Chacombe

Key

▬▬▬ Canal	Built up area	Shops	Pub
······ River	Stations	Accomodation	Restaurant
▥▥▥ Railway	Open water	Campsite	
─ ─ ─ Motorway			
▬▬ A Road			
── B Road			

BASICS

INTRODUCTION

As befits its largely agricultural past, both people and services are well dispersed on this stretch. As with the previous section there's really only one canal-side 'centre', that of Cropredy, which does at least have the advantage over Napton in the previous section of sitting by the water itself.

SHOPPING

As with the section from Napton, there's little to excite the keen shopper along this stretch. Opportunities to gather in supplies are fairly basic with any more exotic needs having to wait for Banbury to be satisfied.

That said, the one real focus of retail activity, Bridge Stores in Cropredy (01295 750987), does offer a comprehensive selection of food and emergency supplies. Located just above Cropredy Lock on the eastern side of the main bridge (Number 153), the shop is a Spar stocking fresh fruit and vegetables as well as local produce, frozen food and freshly baked bread. The cheese counter is worth a browse and the store also has its own ATM. The store also operates lengthy opening hours, including Sunday (although it closes at lunchtime in the winter).

Also within Cropredy is The Green Scene, which sells a selection of crafts (01295 758203) and a Post Office, tucked away in the heart of the village behind the Methodist chapel. Hidden away slightly on the road out of Cropredy towards Claydon is Oathill Farm Supplies (01295 758663), a farm shop offering dry cured bacons and hams as well as sausages and pork and seasonal fruit and vegetables.

There are also a couple of more traditional garden centres, one outside Farnborough (01295 690479) on the A423 and another, the Barn Farm Plant and Garden Centre, in Upper Wardington (01295 758080).

Although not really a retailing operation, Little Bourton is host to the North Oxfordshire Wine Company (01295 750075), which sells not only wine but also custom-made hampers including wine, spirits, cheese, smoked salmon and chocolates.

EATING AND DRINKING

Whilst most of the villages scattered around this stretch may have lost their village shop, most have hung on to their 'local'. Some have survived by evolution, adapting their décor and menu to meet the demands of the transient visitor, whilst others have stuck steadfastly to their roots. In the absence of a shop, and with church attendance declining, it is the pub with its sporting and quiz teams and set of familiar faces that has become the focal point of social activity in these communities.

SECTION B   FENNY COMPTON TO NORTH BANBURY

Above: *Not all the boats along this stretch are luxury leisure craft.*

Opposite above: *The sign at Chipping Warden offers a microcosm of its history.*
Opposite below: *There's no shortage of places to go in Cropredy.*

The Carpenters Arms in Lower Boddington (01327 260451) is unmissable, sitting on the main crossroads in the village, with seats outside to watch the world go by whilst clutching a pint of Hook Norton. The pub's affiliation with this local brew is clearly something they're proud to share as it is painted in large black letters against a white background on the side of the pub.

The Inn at Farnborough, in Farnborough (01295 690615), is a good example of a pub that has set its sights beyond the immediate village market, to the point where its presence now dominates the village centre, rivalling the Hall down the road as the main magnet for visitors. The accent here is on exceptional food and fine wines and the pub, housed in a listed building dating back to 1700, is split up into three 'venues' – the Bar, the Conservatory and the Restaurant. There's a large car park and it is a good place to while away the best part of an afternoon.

By way of contrast, the Griffin (01295 660230) in Chipping Warden still sees itself as the quintessential village local, although this village is unusual along this stretch for being a 'two-pub town'. The Griffin sits in the older half of the village and the Rose and Crown (01295 660216) on the other side of the A361 that bisects it.

The Green Man (01295 750692) sits on the edge of Mollington and provides another good example of a village local, whilst the two pubs in Cropredy, understandably perhaps, have opened their arms to those from outside the village. In neither case however has this involved going down the heavily themed route, and both retain a 'local' atmosphere.

The Brasenose Arms (01295 750244) near the Green offers both food (including the occasional barbeque) as well as bed and breakfast, whilst the Red Lion (01295 750224) near the canal, hidden away in a row of cottages, places a stronger accent on its restaurant, where booking ahead is strongly advised.

> The Brasenose Arms is so named in recognition of the village's strong links with Brasenose College in Oxford, which has owned land in and around the village since 1524.

The Wardingtons, as befits their split-level existence, have two pubs, the busy Hare and Hounds (01295 750645) near the equally busy main road, and the much quieter Plough (01295 750476) in Upper Wardington. Until forty years ago there was a third pub here, the Wheatsheaf, on neutral territory opposite the church, and signs of its former existence can still be seen today.

The Bell Inn is also opposite a church, in this case All Saints in Great Bourton (01295 750504). The pub serves food and was originally thatched and attached to a cottage which stuck out into the road, which is one way of getting fresh customers and of confusing them when they leave! Even more recently than Wardington, Great Bourton had another pub, The Swan, but this has now been converted into offices.

There's another Plough (01295 750222) in Little Bourton, although it actually sits on the edge of the village on the A423, convenient for passing trade. The intriguingly named Moon and Sixpence (01295

730544) in Hanwell combines both a locals' bar and a snug bar with a third restaurant area, which itself exists on a split-level.

The final one-pub village on this stretch is Chacombe, with its George and Dragon (01295 711500), which dates back to the sixteenth century and offers a range of food spanning bar snacks to full restaurant meals.

LUNCHES AND LIGHT BITES
If you're after something other than pub or restaurant food, this section offers two venues for a light snack. The Green Scene in Cropredy (01295 758203) has a tea shop serving homemade pastries and light lunches, which operates alongside its craft gallery (open Tuesday-Saturday). Similarly, the tearoom at the Claydon Bygones Museum (01295 690238) offers a lunchtime blackboard menu of homemade meals and snacks (including puddings!) using seasonal produce. The museum also sells homemade cakes and cream teas in the afternoon.

SLEEPING

HOTELS
This section is not well-endowed with hotels, the closest being the Brasenose Arms in Cropredy (01295 750244), a seventeenth-century inn near the centre of the village offering six en-suite rooms in a converted barn as well as a family room. The sixteenth-century George and Dragon pub in Chacombe (01295 711500) also offers three en-suite rooms. Otherwise the nearest hotel is the Premier Lodge Hotel (0870 990 6512) just outside the area a mile north of Shotteswell on the B4100 next to the Wobbly Wheel pub. This is a thirty-nine room functional hotel belonging to a national chain.

BED AND BREAKFAST/GUESTHOUSES
There are some B&B's and guesthouses, however, although again these are fairly thin on the ground. They include:

- **Poplars Farm**, Cropredy (01295 750561) – *farmhouse B&B with two double rooms. Breakfasts cooked with organic produce.*
- **High Acres**, Great Bourton (01295 750217).
- **Sears Cottage**, Lower Boddington (01327 260271).
- **Point to Point House**, Near Mollington (01295 690346).
- **Red Lion House**, Upper Wardington (01295 758369).
- **Old Bonhams**, Wardington (01295 758069) – *adults only.*
- **Home Farm House**, Williamscot (01295 750500) – *farmhouse B&B with one twin room.*

CAMPING
There are two good campsites:
- **Anita's Touring Caravan Park**, Mollington (01295 750731) – *family run site on edge of village with good facilities for caravans and some tents.*
- **Barnstones**, Great Bourton (01295 750289) – *award-winning site with mix of caravan and tent pitches and excellent amenities.*

SECTION B

SECTION B FENNY COMPTON TO NORTH BANBURY

Opposite above: *Cropredy Lock is one of the most picturesque on the canal.*
Opposite below: *Claydon Middle Lock welcomes another boat.*

Top: *St Mary the Virgin church in Cropredy dates back to the thirteenth century.*
Above: *When in Claydon, take time to examine some of the unusual brickwork.*

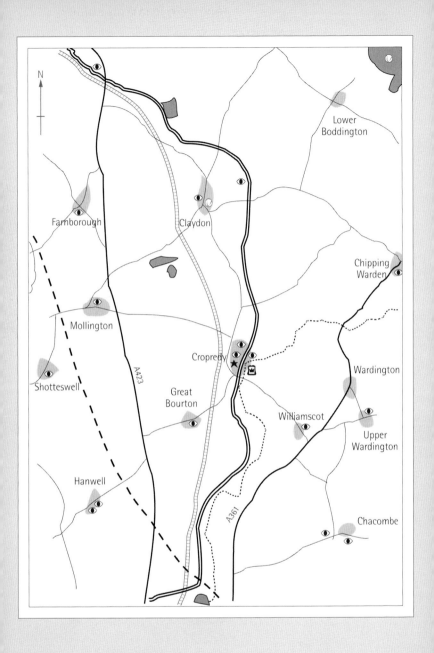

N

Lower
Boddington

Farnborough

Claydon

Chipping
Warden

Mollington

Wardington

Cropredy

Shotteswell

Great
Bourton

Williamscot

Upper
Wardington

A423

Hanwell

A361

Chacombe

Key

—— Canal
········· River
++++++++ Railway
— — Motorway
—— A Road
— B Road

Built up area
Stations
Open water

Site/Sight
Leisure
Entertainment
Culture

SEEING AND DOING

INTRODUCTION

Sights worth a visit along this stretch tend to have a focus on the historical. Most of the villages hereabouts can trace their anteced-ents back to the Domesday Book if not before, and traces of feudal life and the Civil War abound. The relative isolation of each village has also meant that they've had a chance to develop their own character and eccentricities, many of which still manifest in different ways today. The entertainment spotlight tends to shine south towards Banbury, although this section does have one thing Banbury would probably love to have: an annual festival of national (if not international) renown!

SECTION B

SIGHTS

Before straying from the towpath, it is worth noting the disused railway bridge just south of Wormleighton Reservoir which once carried the old Stratford-upon-Avon and Midland Junction Railway (SMJR) before it linked up with the Great Western Railway to the west. This was one of the country's smaller railways and was used mainly to shift freight, notably bananas between South Wales and east London.

> For the few who travelled on its infrequent passenger services, the SMJR became known as the Slow Mouldy and Jolty Railway due to the poor state of its track and rolling stock.

Claydon Bygones Museum (01295 690258) is the sort of place that parents and grandparents take the younger generation in order to dem-onstrate how lucky they are to live in a world of convenience. That and to have the chance to exclaim, 'We used to have one of those!' Opened in 1972 the collection has become a permanent museum and is now owned by the founder's daughter. In truth, dads and granddads might enjoy the place more, as a prominent part of the collection, built up over sixty years by local lad Andrew Fox, is a number of tractors and steam engines – as well as a Sinclair C5. Ten old Banbury shops have been recreated and there is even a 1900 street barrel organ. The museum also serves lunches and teas, and those wandering off the towpath will probably want to devote at least half a day to do it justice.

Before leaving Claydon it's also worth visiting the church. Most of the village churches along this stretch are centuries old and have a story to tell. Claydon's church of St James the Great stands on the highest spot in the village and can date itself back to 1100, although the current structure was restored in 1861. The oldest part of the church is the early English chapel, which is unusual in so small a church and its existence

SECTION B FENNY COMPTON TO NORTH BANBURY

Above: *The church in Great Bourton is one of the few in the country to have a separate bell tower.*

Opposite above: *The Manor House in Wardington suffered badly from a fire in 2004.*
Opposite below left: *Canal artist Jane Selkirk at work.*
Opposite below right: *This pan is an example of the artist's work.*

suggests that someone of importance was once buried here, with the chapel provided for people to pray for their soul. The tower dates back to 1450 and has a saddleback roof with three bells. It was to help raise funds to save this unusual tower that the museum was originally created.

Also near Claydon, in fact in the cottage at Claydon Top Lock, is the workshop of canalware artist Jane Selkirk (01295 690048). Jane's motto is 'if we're in we're open' and if she is it is worth a visit to see her at work and maybe pick up a piece of her ware. Jane paints anything from a wooden spoon to a pair of Hotel boats, so it is probably a good idea not to stand still too long!

> Claydon's church has a clock with no face the steady ticking of which resonates in the small space inside. This is thought to date back to 1572 and to this day it is wound daily by a team of honorary clock keepers.

> The Top Lock Cottage is known as 'The Old Smithy' as it was built in 1815 by the Oxford Canal Company to forge their metal fittings, not as you might expect because there was once a blacksmith here catering to horses pulling the boats.

In a field to the north of Claydon you can also hunt for the Three Shires Stones which supposedly mark the point where Oxfordshire, Northamptonshire and Warwickshire meet.

Between Claydon and Cropredy stands the Grade II Listed Clattercote Priory, once a major landowner and source of influence in this area and beyond. The house was recently sensitively restored and although it is a private residence it is possible to visit the ancient cellars and chapel if you obtain prior permission.

Another notable local building is Farnborough Hall (01295 690002), although the history here goes back 'only' 300 years. What makes that history remarkable however is that it has remained the home of the same family for that period, even though these days it is owned by the National Trust.

> Farnborough's church has a number of memorials to members of the Holbech family, one of whom was a bishop of St Helena.

The house and gardens can be viewed together or separately, although these are not always open at the same time and it is worth phoning ahead for visiting times. The garden was landscaped in the 1740s and has remained largely unchanged with terracing and a series of temples and an obelisk, whilst just outside the house are two large lakes. The house itself is built of honey-coloured stone and is famed for its intricate plasterwork

Over to the east it is worth pausing at Chipping Warden if for no other reason than to look at the old market steps, now positioned in front of the church. Looking a little like a mini-Aztec pyramid, farmers used to position their cattle or produce at the foot of the steps whilst the auctioneer, standing on the top, would inspect the quality of the proffered goods, gauge where to open the bidding and manage the auction accordingly.

Farnborough Hall.

Take a walk around the outside of the church of St Peter and St Paul in order to look at the various gargoyles and intricate plumbing coming off the roof, whilst the thatched Long House and Old Post Office Cottage, also opposite the church, make it possible to imagine how life must once have been in this village (if you took away the cars). There was once a castle here which acted as the baronial home to the lords of Chipping Warden, located in the grounds between the entrance lodge to Edgcott to the southeast and the mansion. There's also a manor house, now a working farm, which was built by the Saltonstall family in the seventeenth century and which has a splendid gateway protecting it off the main road.

In the centre of Chipping Warden there is a village sign, a feature of which is a Second World War bomber. Chipping Warden was one of a string of bomber training bases along the Northamptonshire/ Oxfordshire border and remains one of the best preserved. Others have become private landing strips, farmland or, in the case of Silverstone, a racing circuit. Although it's not possible to visit, the site (now partly occupied by an industrial estate) had three runways set out as an 'A', a perimeter track and thirty-four 'frying pan' hardstandings.

D'Arcy Dalton Way, a road name which asks more questions than it answers, leads up behind a house and up a hill to the church of All Saints in Mollington. Guarded by a set of spiked gates, the church is significant for having an ancient Celtic cross and a stone outhouse where funeral beer used to be stored for those needing more secular assistance to get through an interment.

Altogether more gentle is the only village actually sitting on the canal in this section: Cropredy, although it was not always this way. Over 450 years ago in 1644 the village was the focus of the struggle between the King, Charles I and his rebellious Parliament. The opposing armies spent some time eyeing each other's position on

> Visitors to Cropredy are encouraged to use the sports club car park just over the river bridge, which offers extensive off-street parking.

SECTION C   NORTH BANBURY TO AYHNO

Opposite above: *Lamphreys building, Banbury, still bears the signs of its Victorian advertising.*
Opposite below: *On leaving Banbury the canal quickly becomes engulfed by industrial buildings.*

Top left: *This Victorian post box in the heart of Banbury is a rarity.*
Top right: *The sign for the Great Western Arms in Ayhno leaves no doubt about its rail antecedents*
Above: *Banbury Lock provides a picturesque approach to the town.*

opposite sides of the River Cherwell when, on 29 June, the Parliamentarians led by Sir William Waller sensed that the king's troops were too stretched out and he seized the initiative, crossing the river over Cropredy Bridge and further south at Slat's Mill.

Despite starting well, Waller's men started to lose heavy casualties and important artillery and retreated. Another standoff began, but desertions and poor morale meant that Waller was in no state to chase the king's men when, after two days, they headed back to Oxford. This engagement led to a rethink amongst the Parliamentarians that in time resulted in the formation of Cromwell's New Model Army and the king's nemesis.

The battlefield site remains an open space, and a plaque on the modern bridge marks the spot's significance. Just to the east of the bridge there's another plaque, this time placed just in front of a semi-circular rock by the side of the road. This is an old boundary stone, said to date back to the fifteenth or sixteenth century, which was unearthed in 2001 about 5ft deep in the ground. It was re-erected the following year to mark the Queen's Golden Jubilee.

Coal Wharf, Cropredy.

Cropredy wears its canal heritage proudly, understandably so as the arrival of the canal led to a revival in its fortunes. The turning and water point just below Bridge Stores was once a coal wharf and Cropredy also became something of a centre for brickmaking. Tolls were also collected here, some-

> Just up from the Coal Wharf there is a detailed notice board giving more information on both the Battle of Cropredy and other elements of the village's past, along with a detailed map.

thing that always tends to burn a placename into the collective canal consciousness. The Coal Wharf is remembered as the name of a small arts centre (see below) and the village also has an active canoe club.

Spiritual needs in the village are met by the imposing church of St Mary the Virgin, which dates back to the thirteenth century, along with a Methodist chapel behind it. The old Methodist chapel is now the post office. St Mary's has an old pendulum clock, which can be seen from the nave. By the village

> The south chapel of St Mary's is dedicated to St Fremund, said to be the son of Offa of Mercia.

green there's also the highly weathered remains of a medieval stone cross, which according to the locals has taken on the shape of a cup and saucer (complete with teaspoon), a view reflected in the unusual road name in which it sits. The children's play area also sits on this road behind some garages.

A Cropredy Village Trail is available from the Banbury Tourist Information Centre (see Learn More and Links), and the information board also provides a useful do-it-yourself guide. Mentioned in these is the Old Bakehouse, where villagers would bring their Sunday joint to be roasted right up until the 1930s; Tradesmen's Row, where skilled artisans such as masons, carpenters and saddlers used to congregate; and The Malt House.

> Local tradition says that if a bargee's wife ran into the shoemaker's shop they would be served first so that she could complete her business in the time it took her husband to take their boat through Cropredy Lock.

Wardington is split into two parts each with its own pub, with Lower Wardington dominated by its early English church, which sits on a hill opposite the old Wheatsheaf Inn, which had to close in 1965 due to lack of car parking space. Wardington Manor in Upper Wardington has traditionally been the main focal point of the village. An old Elizabethan manor occupied by Lord Wardington, this was badly damaged by fire in April 2004.

Like many of the village churches along this stretch, All Saints church in Bourton may look as if it has been around since the year dot, but it is in fact only 600 years old. A little over 150 years ago it fell into disrepair, and worshippers were allocated a section of Cropredy church for their use. Whilst the building may have been deemed unsafe for the righteous, it was felt to be okay for children, with the building becoming the local school. The fabric was restored and the building returned to its intended use in 1863. All Saints' other distinguishing feature is its detached stone bell tower with wooden belfry, complete with arch beneath. Reputedly there are only two other places in England where the bell tower is similarly sited away from the church.

As with so many local villages the most distinguishing feature of Shotteswell is its church, St Lawrence. The good folk of Shotteswell seem to have a strong community spirit, coming together to fund a new bus shelter in 1962 and again a few years later to resist British Telecom who wanted to replace their traditional red telephone box with a more modern version. A resistance group blocked the road to the lorry delivering the replacement and the original box now stands defiant on a slight hill.

A Millennium bench also marks out Williamscot near Cropredy, but a stronger claim to fame for this small hamlet is a lone tree in a field 100yds from the A361, which is said to mark the spot where the king made camp during the Battle of Cropredy Bridge. Local lore has it that the present tree is a descendent of the tree that stood then.

On the face of it, Hanwell is simply another ironstone village, and as you approach it from the west the sight of a minimalist wooden village hall may confirm this impression. In fact, there are a number of things about Hanwell to suggest that it exists as a dynamic local community. This feeling is quickly confirmed by a visit to St Peter's church, which can date itself back to the twelfth century, and has two clear distinguishing

SECTION D   AYHNO TO GIBRALTAR

Above: *Bletchingdon church has a separate graveyard protected by this arch.*

Opposite: *The lychgate at Fritwell church, unusually named for St Olaf, the Christian king of Norway.*

features. The first of these is a series of sculptures, male and female figures around the nave pillar capitals, with those on the south side including minstrels playing a range of instruments. Friezes on the external walls of the chancel include a mermaid, two facing warriors and a woman chasing a fox stealing a goose. The second main feature is another faceless clock. An early example of a crown-wheel and berge mechanism, this was designed by the local lord of the manor Sir Anthony Cope in 1671 and was recently restored so that it still strikes the hour – with a little daily correction of the mechanism! The clock is recessed in the East Wall and its pendulum and pulleys, as well as intricate cogs, can be clearly seen and have a somewhat mesmeric quality.

The Cope family in fact go back a long way in Hanwell, with William Cope, onetime Cofferer to King Henry VII, responsible for starting the building of Hanwell Castle in 1498, which can be seen from the church. Perhaps the most famous inhabitant of the castle

A survivor, Anthony Cope went on to become a favourite of King James I, who he entertained twice at the castle in 1605 and 1611. An alabaster monument exists to him and his wife, as well as their ten children, in the church.

was Sir Anthony Cope (a forebearer of the one who designed the clock). A leading Puritan, Sir Anthony tried to introduce a Puritan version of the prayer book into the House of Commons and enjoyed a spell in the Tower of London for his efforts in 1587.

In fact, Hanwell's castle was a fortification in name only, being more of a castellated manor house. Most of the building was demolished in the eighteenth century with the remains being used as a farmhouse. The south-west tower and south wing survive, however, along with five ornamental fishponds, and at the time of writing the tower was being restored.

Other testaments to Hanwell's sense of community spirit include its green, which has a rock garden and bench, and its community observatory. Sited in the grounds of the castle, this facility boasts amongst other telescopes a 30in reflector and is periodically open to members of the public.

An earth mound in Berry Close in Chacombe is thought to cover the remains of a fortified Norman manor house, but the only two surviving buildings of any significance today are the church and Chacombe Priory. The latter is a mansion set back from the road in from the A361 and is surrounded by woodland and a lake. The

Chacombe church rather cheekily put in an insurance claim for war damage by enemy action to the diocese. The stained glass was eventually replaced by plain.

Priory has been a private house since 1545, but evidence of its former use as an Augustine retreat includes a mediaeval chapel.

Although Chacombe was touched by the Civil War, a more recent conflict left its mark on both the Priory and the church. A stray bomb from the raid on Coventry in November 1940 felled part of the Priory's wall and shattered stained glass in the church. Shards of this glass were to turn up fifty years later in a Deddington antique shop.

Chacombe Priory.

Other places of interest off the map but nearby include the National Herb Centre in Warmington (01295 690999), which has over 500 different herb varieties, with examples of many offered for sale.

If repeated mention of the Civil War has excited an interest to learn more you may also wish to visit the Radway Tower on the summit of Edgehill, north-west of Banbury on the A429. This Octagonal Tower, now an inn, marks the spot where King Charles I raised his standard on 23 October 1642 before the first major battle of the English Civil War. The tower was started in 1742 to commemorate the 100th anniversary of the battle and opened on 3 September 1750, the anniversary of Oliver Cromwell's death.

CULTURE

Although this section may appear to exist in a cultural vacuum between Banbury to the south and Warwickshire to the north, it can lay claim to the annual Cropredy Festival, known locally as 'Fairports' as it features the annual reunion of the members of the folk group Fairport Convention.

Whilst folk music is the predominant theme, in recent years the festival has branched out a little. Held in the second weekend in August from Thursday to Sunday, most festival goers tend to camp and those with canal boats become the gentry. The event is organised by a member of Fairport Convention and a combination of domestic crises and age mean that every year may be the last so if you are interested it is worth catching whilst you can.

ENTERTAINMENT

Cropredy also has its own Arts Club at the Old Coal Wharf (01295 750878), which also has a cinema capable of seating twenty-five and is available for private hire, although it does run a regular programme.

Most of the villages in this section have some kind of play area for children, of varying levels of complexity.

SECTION D   AYHNO TO GIBRALTAR

Below: *Heyford Wharf, opposite the railway station, is a popular spot for hire boats.*

Right: *Somerton Deep Lock is well named, being 12ft deep.*

Opposite below: *Pollarded willows line the bankside after the Heyfords.*

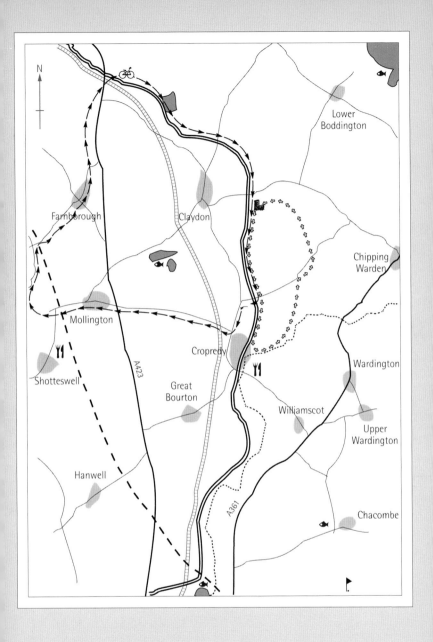

Key

━━━ Canal		Built up area	🚲 ➡ Cycling route/outlet
···· River	● Stations		🥾 ⇨ Walking route/outlet
⊞⊞⊞ Railway		Open water	🐟 Fishing spot/outlet
▬ ▬ Motorway			
━━━ A Road			
─── B Road			

∩ Riding outlet

▶ Golf course/outlet

SAMPLING

INTRODUCTION

After the intricate avoidance of Shirne Hill west of Wormleighton the canal weaves a more relaxed path, dropping 30ft east of Claydon before striking south to join the River Cherwell at Cropredy. Only the latter can truly be said to have a canal-side location, although Claydon comes close, and as such access to the waterway is limited. Combine this with the relative paucity of footpaths in this section and it can be difficult to wander away from the towpath to sample the local landscape.

Walk B has been designed to provide such an opportunity, but otherwise the visitor can probably best sample the many delights offered in this northernmost triangle of Oxfordshire by car or bike. Alternatively, the two large reservoirs created to feed the canal offer good spots to sit and appreciate the rural isolation that characterises this stretch.

The OS Explorer Map covering this stretch is number 206, Edge Hill and Fenny Compton.

WALKING

Other than the towpath the east–west Macmillan Way heading down the towpath to Claydon Locks and then to points east is the main formal path in this section. This can be accessed at either of those two villages or from a parking spot just east of the canal near Bridge 145. Also worthy of note is the Jurassic Way, which follows as a north–south path along the eastern edge of the map just to the east of Wardington.

Other than the bridleways detailed below, other footpaths are thin on the ground, although there are two heading north out of Farnborough

> The 290-mile Macmillan Way links the coasts of Lincolnshire and Dorset with its Cross-Cotswold section stretching from Banbury to Bath. Sponsored walks along the route have raised over £200,000 for Macmillan Nurses.

and others heading north, west and east out of Cropredy, with the latter linking with Wardington, which acts as something of a node point for a network of local paths.

Cherwell District Council produces a useful leaflet detailing both a village trail within Cropredy and a circular 4.5-mile 'Battlefield Walk' taking in both a section of the canal and some of the footpaths around Wardington and Williamscot. This can be obtained from the Tourist Information Centre in Banbury (see Learn More and Links).

Walk B starts at the parking spot mentioned already and heads south down the towpath to Cropredy. On meeting the River Cherwell it heads out over the fields past Prescote Manor to link up with the Macmillan Way, giving the walker a good chance to sample both the canal and

SECTION E   GIBRALTAR TO OXFORD

Above: *Kidlington Dovecote is one of the many gems hidden away in the otherwise modern-looking village.*

Opposite above: *All that remains of Hampton Gay, once a thriving community.*
Opposite below: *Those entering a canal from the Thames are warned that the waterway comes under a different jurisdiction.*

a sense of the farming heritage of this part of the country. The walk includes a fairly steep climb but this is deliberate in order to provide the walker with a good view over the Cherwell Valley and down towards the canal and as such the opportunity to take in a large proportion of the landscape covered in this section.

SECTION B

SECTION B WALK

From Claydon Middle Lock to Cropredy and Back

Description:	*A good stretch out through the heart of this section and over fields.*
Distance:	*5.5 miles*
Duration:	*2 hrs*
Staring point:	*Grid Reference 466499, OS Explorer 206*
Nearest Refreshment:	*Either the Red Lion or the Brasenose Arms at Cropredy.*

Head south from the parking area over the bridge at Claydon Middle Lock and follow the canal past the last of the short flight and, in time, Clattercote Wharf and a series of further locks before entering the long stretch into Cropredy, where the locals with canal-side gardens all seem to have green fingers.

At Cropredy Lock head up the path by the side of the bridge and turn left down the road where the River Cherwell makes its first appearance on your right. Bear right and up past the impressive Prescote Manor and pick up the footpath over a stile in the field on your left just after the drive. Follow this north-east, keeping with the direction of the road, aiming to the left of the farm. Just before the farm another path cuts in front and you need to take this left (north-west).

Follow this path until you reach a road where you turn right and head uphill to Highfield Farm, about a mile. Just after the cowshed pick up signs on your left for the Macmillan Way, entering a field. Keep with the boundary to a metal gate and go through this, sticking with the boundary to the right-hand corner of the following field. The path then heads sharply downhill past some woods and straight over two subsequent fields, meeting a sign half way down the left-hand boundary of the second.

Continue to the corner of this field and then straight on in the next. At the bottom of the hill, where there is a corner in the field, take the bridge into the field on your left and follow this half-right back to your starting point.

The best place to go for walking equipment and supplies is Banbury (see Section C).

CYCLING

The extreme north and south of the towpath provide very solid paths for cycling this stretch, with the former offering the chance to explore the Fenny Compton Tunnel and the latter the last stretch of rural calm before Banbury. There are plenty of access points to the canal along this stretch, with the parking at Claydon and off the A423 outside Fenny Compton favourites. Cropredy also provides a natural focal point as does Banbury.

There are also plenty of side roads to construct circular routes, allowing the cyclist to avoid the busy trunk roads that emanate out from Banbury and define this area. One suggested route of around 15 miles takes in many of the villages covered in this section but be aware that it is hilly in parts.

Start at the parking on the A423 by Bridge 137a, and follow the towpath south-east and then due south to Broadmoor Bridge (Number 150). Turn right here and then left, heading for Cropredy but turning right onto Oxhey Hill just before it. Follow this road to and through Mollington, taking care when crossing the A423.

Take the March Road until it meets a T-junction where you turn right onto the Mollington Road. Before entering Warmington turn right towards Farnborough. Turn right at the next T-junction and then through Farnborough itself. Locate the gated road to Fenny Compton halfway down Windmill Hill (The Slade). After about a mile take the footpath on the right, which takes you back to the canal. Go over the bridge and you'll be back at your starting point

The best place to look for bike supplies along this stretch is Banbury (see Section C).

RIDING

Public bridleways along this stretch include three short stretches heading to the east and south of Farnborough, including one heading towards Claydon, as well as a longer path linking that village to the Wormleighton Reservoir. Another path leads north from Cropredy along the Claydon Road before heading across country to link with a minor road that takes you to Lower Boddington. Another short path heads north of Williamscot before splitting east–west, with the latter linking back into the Claydon Road via Broadmoor Bridge over the canal, giving the rider a short circular route.

> The British Horse Society also produce a book offering twenty-two routes within South Warwickshire and parts of Northamptonshire, many of which cut through this section. They can be contacted on 08701 202244.

Equestrian Suppliers along this stretch include:
• **The Valley Farm Equestrian Centre** on the Shotteswell/Mollington road (01295 730576), *which offers riding lessons and hacks.*

SECTION E GIBRALTAR TO OXFORD

Above: *One of the best ways to appreciate the Oxford skyline is from the top of one of the towers open to the public.*

Opposite above: *One of the many alleyways you can lose yourself in in Oxford.*
Opposite below: *The canal's final lock and effectively its terminus.*

FISHING

This section is well served with fishing spots. Canal fishing is controlled by the following:

- **Banbury and District AA**
  – Banbury to Cropredy.
- **Standard-Triumph Recreation Club**
  – Cropredy Lock to Bridge 148.

- **Sphinx** – *Bridge 148 to Claydon*
- **Ford (Leamington) AC** – *Claydon to Fenny Compton.*

In addition, a number of lakes are available to the casual and club angler alike. These include:

- **Chacombe Fishery**, Chacombe just south of Williamscot to the west of the A361 (01295 750115) – *Lake with carp, roach, bream and tench, open dawn to dusk.*
- **Clattercote Reservoir**, off the road linking Claydon with the A423 (01295 270796) – *Lake surrounded by a wooden walkway with 122 jetty-style pegs. This arrangement has made the lake more fishable and allowed the retention of much of the local habitat. A mixed coarse*

fishery with an emphasis on carp (up to 25lbs), tench up to 7lb, chub and bream up to 3lb and roach and perch up to 2lb. Pike and tench are also caught regularly. Try and get pegs 90-110.

- **Drayton Leisure Centre Fishing Lake**, to the north east of Banbury (01295 730242) – *Lake also with a wooden walkway with carp, tench, rudd, bream and roach, open dawn to dusk. The centre also has a snack bar and toilets.*

WATER SPORTS

Banbury Sailing Club is an active user of the Boddington Reservoir and has a large boathouse on the water's edge. Members sail for fun or race most weekends, making full use of the 90 acres of water at their disposal in either their own boats or those owned by the club, which include Toppers and Optimists

The Banbury and District Canoe Club is a privately run members' club in Cropredy (01295 730611), situated on the canal near Cropredy Lock. It has a good stock of equipment including club boats and regularly gets involved in both Marathon and Sprint racing as well as tours of different waterways.

OTHER

For the golfer there are two courses, both to the north of Banbury but just within the area covered by the map. These are:

- **Drayton Leisure Centre** (01295 730242) – *9 holes, 913yds. A useful par-three course which also has a twelve-bay floodlit driving range and a shop. Snacks are also available.*
- **Cherwell Edge Golf Club** (01295 711591) – *18 holes, 5,947yds. This also has a floodlit practice range and putting green as well as a pro-shop and clubhouse.*

SECTION C

NORTH BANBURY TO AYHNO

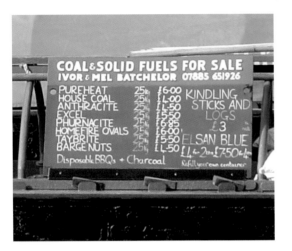

COAL & SOLID FUELS FOR SALE
IVOR & MEL BATCHELOR 07885 651926

PUREHEAT	25kg	£6·00
HOUSE COAL	25kg	£6·00
ANTHRACITE	25kg	£6·50
EXCEL	25kg	£5·50
PHURNACITE	25kg	£6·85
HOMEFIRE OVALS	25kg	£6·00
TAYBRITE	25kg	£5·50
BARGE NUTS	25kg	£4·50

KINDLING
STICKS AND
LOGS
£3
ELSAN BLUE
£4·2ltr £7·50 4ltr

Disposable BBQs + Charcoal

Refill your own container

SECTION E   GIBRALTAR TO OXFORD

Above left: *Coal can still be bought from water tradesmen at Thrupp.*
Above right: *Thrupp is best visited on a sultry sunny day.*

Below left: **Dawn** *and* Dusk, *a pair of hotel boats moored at Thrupp.*
Below right: *These sculptures offer a poetic insight into the canal at Thrupp..*

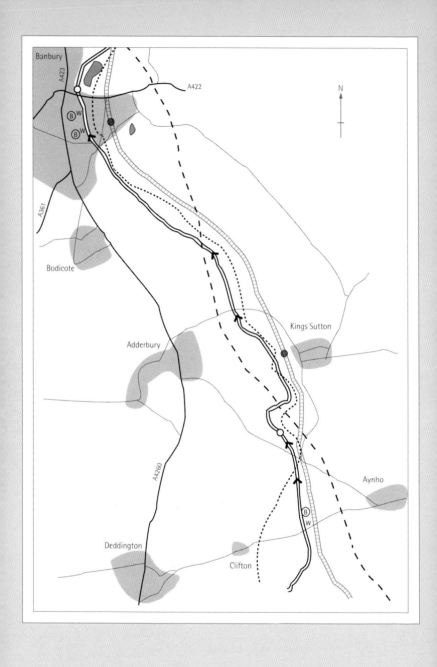

Banbury
A423
A422
B W
B W
A361
Bodicote
Adderbury
A4260
Kings Sutton
Aynho
B W
Deddington
Clifton

N

Key

Canal		Built up area	○	Turning point
River		Stations		Lock
Railway		Open water	ⓑ	Boatyard
Motorway			W	Waterpoint
A Road				

SHAPERS

THE CANAL ON THIS STRETCH

KEY FACTS

LENGTH: 7.5 miles

BOATYARDS: 3
- Sovereign Narrowboats
- Tooleys Boatyard
- Ayhno Wharf

WATERPOINTS: 3
- Sovereign Narrowboats
- Tooleys Boatyard
- Ayhno Wharf

TURNING POINTS: 4
- Grimsbury Wharf
- Banbury Tramway
- Nell Bridge
- Ayhno Wharf

LOCKS: 6
- Hardwick Bridge (7ft 62in)
- Banbury (5ft 10in)
- Grant's (9ft 6in)
- Kings Sutton (10ft 8in)
- Nell Bridge (8ft 8in)
- Aynho Weir (1ft 0in)

Beginning and ending with rural scenes, this stretch of the canal is dominated by Banbury, which, having taken a long time to arrive peters out relatively quickly once the centre is passed through. Back amongst the open fields this section is distinguished by its proliferation of lift bridges, but the locks are evenly spread out, making for steady progress.

From Hardwick Lock the canal passes under the railway and enters a long straight stretch, which ends with a bend to the left by an eggshell-blue painted cottage. Long-term and overnight moorings are offered here, but you are still some way out of town. Banbury's imminence is heralded by the smell of coffee roasting in the unseen factories on the estate on the opposite bank. The footpath is pretty solid here and the walking easy.

After another straight the canal passes under the A422 and a branch of the Cherwell comes alongside. The old branch to Grimsbury Wharf appears and offers a turning point, but visibility isn't wonderful so boaters need to take care. This marks the beginning of some long-term moorings with Spiceball Park to the left. After Bridge 163 the towpath becomes gravelled and another straight brings you into the outskirts of Banbury proper, with the long-term moorings becoming first 14 day and then 48 hour before counting down into the short-term 24-hour variety.

There is a children's playground in the parkland at this point opposite Sovereign Narrowboats, a boatyard with somewhat erratic opening hours. Look up and you may just see the distinctive pepper-pot roof of St Mary's church on the skyline to the right. The towpath is made of brick as you enter Banbury town centre, marked first by the Tom Rolt Bridge and then by the modernity of the Castle Quay shopping mall, where there's also the Castle Quay Café right on the side of the canal. There is plenty of mooring along here but it can get busy in summer.

Tom Rolt bridge plaque, Banbury.

Passing through Banbury Lock brings you down alongside the railway station and its line of blue railings. There are further 48-hour moorings here, although you need to take pot luck with the state of the bank. These end by Bridge 168, where there is easy access to a Morrison's supermarket on the opposite bank. Banbury Tramway long-term moorings follow and end with another turning point. There's a park on the right-hand bank but sadly it is inaccessible

> Tom Rolt Bridge commemorates the sixtieth anniversary of the journey of 'Cressy' that led first to a book and in time to the formation of the Inland Waterways Association.

from this side. The towpath continues in good condition as Banbury's housing recedes and emerges quickly into flat open fields with lift bridges over the canal, not all of which may be raised!

From Nadkey Bridge (172) there are stretches offering good mooring, but be aware of occasional bank slips and patches of weed. The not-so distant hum of the motorway begins to impose itself around here, along with the smell of the animal feed processing plant in the impressive mill on the Cherwell to the east.

Grants Lock is a deep one and guarded by a recently renovated cottage. There is a long stretch of good mooring between Stevens Lift Bridge (176) and Twyford Wharf (177) and beyond, although south of the bridge it can become congested with permanently moored craft. Although a pleasant place to stop, there's not a lot within walking distance. If you are so

Ayhno Moorings.

minded however you can pause to take in the sign on the bridge warning traction engine drivers to take it easy. Twyford Wharf is also the home of the cheesily-named Twilite Moorings and Caravan Park.

The towpath can get a bit slippery here for cyclists and is not wide enough to make too many mistakes. After Kings Sutton Lock there are a few mooring opportunities, but these need to be judged with care as old bank stones have slipped into the water and there is a fair bit of silting. The sound of the motorway also begins to encroach. From Bridge 182 it's possible to look out over the meadows of the Cherwell to Kings Sutton Station where the imposing spire of the village's church dominates the horizon for a while.

The Cherwell itself soon makes a brief reappearance alongside the canal but disappears when the latter bends sharp right to go under the M40. The long straight stretch up to Nell Bridge that soon follows has some good mooring and is relatively quiet. A bend leading up to the lock next to the bridge offers both a turning point and the sight of a number of beached boats on the gravel to the right, as well as a splendid lock-keeper's cottage.

Those not on a boat should take care crossing the busy road, where there is a long lay-by – handy if you are in a car. A long stretch of good towpath leads to the meeting of the canal and river, so boaters need to be aware of a possible pull to the right. There is a lock at either end of this stretch and those wielding windlasses may be tempted to walk the few hundred yards between them. The southernmost lock, Ayhno Weir, is an unusual lozenge shape, designed this way to help send sufficient water down to Oxford.

From this point the railway rather than river tends to dominate and the towpath can become less even and even overgrown in summer, with plenty of brambles to provide cyclists with punctures. The stretch ends with the boatyard at Ayhno Wharf, which also has a small shop. The Great Western Arms lies just to the west of the Ayhno's old railway station and from this point on the railway will never be far away.

PRINCIPAL TOWNS AND VILLAGES
ON THIS STRETCH

ADDERBURY
Adderbury's main drag lies to the west of the Oxford Road and the tall spire of the village's impressive church leads the eye right down it. A mixture of thatched and slate roofed cottages in local stone, with the added attraction of four pubs, makes this a good place to pause.

AYHNO
The house and grounds of Ayhnoe Park dominate this small village, which stretches out along the roads linking both Deddington and Adderbury to the A43 and the motorway.

BANBURY
The second largest settlement on the South Oxford after the university city itself. Now a thriving market town with a strong industrial base, Banbury has endured a series of highs and lows over the years. Recent investment has been sympathetic and concentrated along the east end of the town by the canal. The town tends to sprawl a bit, but this is half of its charm, with lots of medieval alleyways meaning it is easy to get lost, but also providing plenty of opportunities for serendipitous discoveries.

BODICOTE
Bodicote has a long main street of honey-coloured terraces with high walls and hedges hiding the occasional larger manor house or ex-merchant's dwelling. Off this there are more modern housing estates and the village seems to be fighting a losing battle not to become a suburb of Banbury.

Adderbury High Street.

SECTION C

Ayhnoe Park.

DEDDINGTON

Deddington was originally destined to be a town in its own right, but never quite escaped Banbury's shadow, although it had its own market until the 1830s. The village centre, a pull off the Oxford Road, contains an eclectic mix of shops and businesses clustered around a market square. The village continues to wear its pride on its sleeve, with plenty of information boards and a coat of arms granted as recently as 1994.

KINGS SUTTON

A straggling village with a distinguished past that can be easily missed but is well worth a visit. Of all the local villages, Kings Sutton is probably the one that shows most signs of recent growth, although thankfully not enough to spoil it, possibly because it is the only village with its own railway station and links into London and Birmingham.

HISTORY

It would be a mistake to think that the history of this area is Banbury's history. Banbury is perhaps the archetypal market town, dependent upon the villages surrounding it to both supply and buy the goods it traded. The relationship between them therefore was one of inter-dependence rather than domination, and many of the villages to the south of Banbury retain a sense of community spirit forged over the centuries.

In fact, it is only relatively recently in historical terms that Banbury has assumed the position of clear local dominance that it enjoys today. Its rise has not been a smooth one, leaving space for the settlements in its southern hinterland to grow and carve their own identity. Indeed, many of the natural advantages enjoyed by the town have not been ones it has enjoyed exclusively. These include proximity to the River Cherwell, and in modern times its access to the canal; along with its position on the road to Oxford.

Banbury itself began to become recognised as a settlement in its own right in Saxon times, although

> One of the cafés in the town has taken the name of 'Banesberie'.

there is plenty of evidence of Roman occupation too. It is recorded in the Domesday Book as 'Banesberie' but its first burst of growth had to wait until the first half of the twelfth century when Alexander, who was both bishop of Lincoln and lord of Banbury, built a castle, created a market and probably also built the first church. This was one of a rash of similar medieval churches in the area at the time, with those at Adderbury and Kings Sutton deemed to have been of at least equal stature.

Around this time Deddington to the south of Banbury was undergoing its own period of growth. Settled around the same time, the last Saxon lord's house was replaced shortly after the Norman Conquest by a castle, occupied by the powerful lord-bishop Odo of Bayeux, who, as his name suggests, was related to the new king. Odo's other main claim to fame was as the commissioner of the tapestry named after his home town. Within a couple of hundred years the castle had largely disappeared and the settlement was laid out as a prototype new town by the pioneering de Chesney family, who now owned the village, although it never really took off as an urban community.

Adderbury was also doing quite well about this time, with the church being rebuilt in the early fifteenth century at a cost of £400, and a school for fifty boys being established towards the end of the 1500s. Kings Sutton's church also dates back to this period and Ayhno was equally establishing an identity for itself around this time. Some of the limestone cottages around today can be dated back to the fifteenth century, with one having a 60ft well dated 1500.

> Banbury cakes were made famous in the eigtheenth century by Betty White. Packed in Chip Willow baskets, they were sold at Banbury Fair, and even as far as America and Australia. In an act of retail irony lamented even at the time, the original cake shop was demolished to make way for the modern Castle Quay development.

By the beginnings of the seventeenth century the local economy was doing well, with Banbury's market making it the natural focal point of activity. Banbury became famous for its cakes, cheese (which was particularly popular in London) and ale. Some semblance of the cakes remain today, but don't bother asking for Banbury cheese as no record remains of what made it distinctive. Ale lived on into modern times, with Hunt Edmonds,

> Beer is still brewed today at the micro-brewery in Bodicote (see 'Basics') and at the famous Hook Norton Brewery 8 miles south-west of Banbury.

the last local brewery, finally succumbing to takeover in 1972, after which the town lost both its vast brewery and a local landmark.

If things were looking good as the new century dawned, the appearance turned out to be a mirage. The events that were to transform the fortunes of the town were about to take place and cast it into a period of prolonged depression. The town began to become known for its puritanical zeal, and the 1600s began with the famous Banbury Cross being destroyed as a symbol of superstition. Some felt that the Great Fire of Banbury which followed in 1628, destroying a third of the town in its wake, was further evidence of an excess of sin amongst the locals, but worse was still to come.

Banbury's strategic position gave it a high profile in the Civil War and the town lost Alexander's castle in the fighting. In fifty short years Banbury was transformed from a prosperous market town to a place mainly covered by ruins, so much so that its people had to petition Parliament (successfully) for permission to use bricks from the castle to rebuild their town.

The surrounding villages also suffered during this period. Strategically placed between Oxford and Banbury they were frequently used to quarter troops and Charles I even slept in Deddington in 1644 and in Ayhno after the battle of Edgehill. Royalist troops continued to occupy Ayhno's manor until the end of the Civil War, at which point they repaid their hosts by burning the place down. The village was lucky however in that Charles II paid compensation to the owners, the Cartwright family, after whom the local hotel is named today. The church was also so badly damaged that it soon fell into disrepair and eventually collapsed.

Five years later Deddington was home to leveller troops, whose fervent views caused alarm even amongst their leaders. Somehow though, Deddington and villages like it managed to avoid the destruction that befell Banbury, helped no doubt by famous patrons. Sir William Scroggs for example, Lord Chief Justice in the latter half of the century, is thought to have been born in Deddington.

It took the rest of the century for Banbury to recover, but by 1700 a new industry was providing some prosperity – textiles. The main products were horse girths and blankets and, in time, a new material originally known as shag but which eventually became known as plush. This was a worsted-based material, with the base cloth woven in surrounding villages and then raised through the use of brass wires before being neatly trimmed off. All sorts of things were made out of plush such as waistcoats and saddles, but it is perhaps best known for its use on servants' uniforms. By 1831 about 550 men were employed to make it on their own looms – some living 12 miles away.

In 1816 Thomas Colley, a Banbury baker, accepted a bid to walk 1,020 miles over twenty consecutive days. He accomplished the feat mainly by getting up around 3 a.m. and covering 30-40 miles before breakfast. When he re-entered the town he was met with huge crowds proclaiming his achievement. His glory was short lived, however, as he died soon after.

Textiles continued to provide a manufacturing component to the local economy for the best part of two centuries, but Banbury's most important role was as a classic market town. Pretty much self-sufficient in most things, its 'exports' of textiles and ale, not to mention cakes and possibly cheese too, meant the town began to become relatively prosperous.

By the nineteenth century the canal was winding its way through the heart of the town, and Banbury began to make a name for itself producing agricultural ironworks, a famous name from this era being that of the Britannia Ironworks, as coke, sand and iron were brought into the town by water.

> William Bowler, inventor of the famous hat, is thought to have been a Deddington resident, as was Mr Harris, better known for his sausages.

As the century progressed the town also gained a reputation for printing. The earliest works were those of John Cheney and a Cheney and Sons still exists in the town today. Meanwhile, the plush industry had hit terminal decline, losing out to Coventry where the machines for converting the raw material into the smooth plush were made. By 1893 there were only 100 full-time textile workers left in Banbury and the last plush factory closed in 1909, although the material continued to be made for another forty years at Shutford, west of Banbury.

Industrial activity was not confined to Banbury during this time however. Adderbury was involved in both cloth and brick making whilst Deddington paper mill supplied the constant need for paper amongst the academics of Oxford. Agriculture was still most households' mainstay however, even if many would also get involved in glove or lace making during the lean winter months.

As with many similar towns however, this growth came at a price and an 1849 enquiry into public health in the town found conditions 'perhaps as extreme... as to be found in the filthiest and most crowded towns of England.' Not a lot was done to improve matters as the local economy stalled during the latter part of the century and many of the fit and able young families emigrated out of the area as first weaving then the ironworks struggled to find markets.

> In 1851 the Inspector of Prisons declared that Banbury's gaol, which had existed since 1558 was 'the worst he'd ever seen'. The Town Council tried to raise the money to rebuild it, but failed.

> The aluminium factory that made Banbury a target had in fact just been fitted out before the war with new machinery – designed by German engineers!

> Whole housing estates would supply the Birds factory with workers, to an extent that one in particular became known as 'the aviary'.

Banbury entered another period of stagnation, this time lasting about fifty years until the Northern Aluminium Company arrived in 1925, bringing a number of new jobs with it. This development was matched in importance by the creation of the cattle market, a sign that the rural side of the local economy remained significant.

The Second World War saw the town regain some of its former position. The town was seen as 'safe' and was the destination for a number of London evacuees. This was despite the presence of the aluminium works which by then was busy making essential specialist parts for allied aircraft, which made the town an occasional target for enemy bombers. Another of their targets may have been Spencer's Corsets, which had been converted to produce vital parts for parachutes.

In the 1950s and '60s many of the near slums were cleared and replaced with new estates. These in turn supplied many of the workers for Alfred Bird and Sons, manufacturers of custard and coffee – a smell which still lingers over the town today. Birds became General Foods and their sports and social club sits alongside the canal near the town centre. Other food scents often on the wind in Banbury include biscuits and bread and these are particularly strong coming into the town along the towpath from the north.

Banbury was now entering its modern age. Like the canal before it, the new M40 linking Coventry and London (not unlike the canal, which did the same via Oxford and the Thames) served to highlight the town's useful position halfway between London and Birmingham, a position confirmed by the revamped Chiltern Railways which upgraded its line in the 1990s. By 1998 the cattle market, which by that time was said to be Europe's largest, was closed down.

Today the town retains its connection with the food industry, but the industrial estates on its periphery near the motorway also play host to a number of factories supplying the motor racing industry and the nearby Silverstone racing circuit. The villages to the south of the town continue to supply Banbury with workers, although they are possibly more likely to be white than blue collar.

Today, these villages are a mix of old and new housing, all of which is regarded as highly desirable. Sufficient strength of community spirit seems to have survived for them to assimilate 'newcomers' without too much dilution of this spirit, and they retain their essential character.

SECTION C

| The popularity of 'Ride a Cock Horse' is due mainly to the Rusher family of Banbury who were one of the first publishers of small books of verse called Chapbooks. | *Ride a cock horse to Banbury Cross,*
To see a fine lady upon a white horse,
With rings on her fingers and
*   bells on her toes,*
She shall have music where-ever
*   she goes* |

It is impossible to close a section on local history without touching upon the rhyme that has made Banbury famous. Some have speculated that the 'Fine Lady' of the nursery rhyme may have been Lady Godiva, who lived in relatively nearby Coventry, or even Elizabeth I, although this seems unlikely! Another candidate is Celia Fiennes, sister of the third Viscount Saye of nearby Broughton Castle. Much more likely is the somewhat more prosaic explanation that it was a local girl who rode in a May Day procession.

The 'cock horse' referred to in the rhyme is in fact a child's hobby horse – in medieval times two people riding on one such horse were said to be riding a 'cock horse' – and the one cross mentioned in the rhyme isn't the one we can see today. The present cross was erected in 1859 to celebrate the marriage of Queen Victoria's eldest daughter to Prince Frederic of Prussia and at the time was not universally welcomed due to the unpopularity of the royal family at the time.

> In 1927 the cross was in danger of being pulled down and an article was published in the *Chicago Herald* appealing to American children to write to the mayor to save it, promising to visit the town when they grew up if he did.

Neo-Gothic in design, the cross is 52.5ft high and two gas lamps were installed shortly after its erection to stop people bumping into it on foggy nights.

THE NATURAL LANDSCAPE

The River Cherwell is a regular companion along this stretch, with its valley providing a natural hollow for the canal to follow. Usually to the east of the canal, the Cherwell crosses the canal at the southern end of the stretch and then disappears for a while to the west, popping up again in Section D. The

> The area around Banbury was chosen to represent a typical rural area in the 1944 Government film *24 Square Miles*.

River Sor passes to the south of Bodicote and flows into the Cherwell just south of Nell Bridge. Elsewhere, there are numerous small springs flowing into these two rivers.

Either side of the Cherwell Valley the land rises up, with Kings Sutton nestling between hills either side of it, with its westernmost point marked by its railway station, which looks out over meadows to the canal, a view which can be appreciated from Bridge 182. Both Aynho and Deddington sit on slight hills, giving some decent views over the valley, whilst Adderbury is more isolated, with the Oxford Road forming an artificial barrier pulling it away from the water.

ACCESS AND TRANSPORT

ROADS

This is perhaps one of the most accessible stretches of the route. The M40 motorway crosses the canal twice in this section, and junctions off the motorway at each end allow access easy for those approaching the canal from a distance. Junction 11 brings you into the heart of Banbury, whilst Junction 10 lies just 2 miles to the south of Ayhno via Souldern and the B4100.

SECTION C

This road links up with the historic Banbury to Oxford road, now known less evocatively as the A4260, at Adderbury, where it traces a route along the west of the canal. Less than a mile north of Adderbury, a minor road heads east, crossing the motorway, canal and River Cherwell in turn before reaching Kings Sutton where another minor road heads north offering an alternative route into Banbury.

RAIL

Both Banbury and Kings Sutton lie on the Chiltern Line linking Marylebone and Birmingham, although the latter is not a major halt. Otherwise, National Train Enquiries can be reached on 08457 484950.

BUSES

Banbury Bus Station is conveniently located right alongside the canal in the heart of the town. The X59 service links Banbury and Oxford and plies the Oxford Road, offering good access to the canal from the west. Local buses linking Deddington, Adderbury, Kings Sutton and Ayhno also run, although timetables should be checked first.

It was a plan to build a new bus station that first led to the local council drawing up plans to fill in the canal in the 1950s, an aspiration that was stifled by the famous boat rally of 1955.

- Stagecoach (01865 772250) *for* X59 *and* Route 499 *Banbury-Twyford-Kings Sutton-Ayhno.*
- Walters Limousines (01235 510959) *for* Route 159/259 *Adderbury-Deddington and points to Steeple Aston.*

- Traveline (www.traveline.org.uk) on 0870 6082608 can give details of specific services between 7 a.m. and 10 p.m.

TAXIS

A selection of the many taxi firms serving this section:
- 1st Union Taxis, Banbury Railway Station (01295 275050).
- 1st A1 Taxis of Banbury (01295 272020).
- Banbury Taxi Co. West Bar Street, Banbury (01295 273333).

- Castle Cars, Banbury Railway Station (01295 270011).
- Halls Cars, Deddington (01869 338759).
- Picketts Cars, Adderbury (01295 812277).

SECTION C

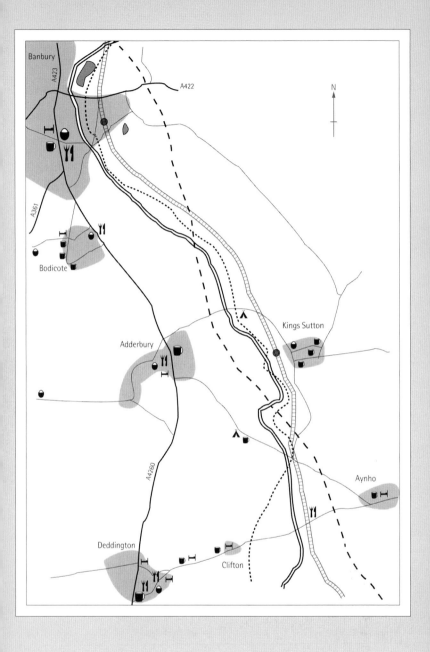

Banbury

A423

A361

A422

N

Bodicote

Adderbury

Kings Sutton

A4260

Aynho

Deddington

Clifton

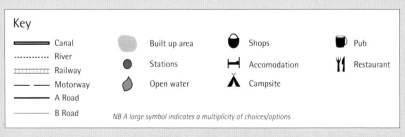

Key

━━━ Canal	▨ Built up area	◗ Shops	▤ Pub
·········· River	◗ Stations	⊢ Accomodation	¶¶ Restaurant
▥▥▥ Railway	◊ Open water	⋀ Campsite	
━ ━ Motorway			
━━━ A Road			
── B Road	*NB A large symbol indicates a multiplicity of choices/options*		

BASICS

INTRODUCTION

Banbury represents both the rough halfway point of the canal as well as a natural focus for commerce and services, including a hospital on the Oxford Road. The town offers an oasis of shops, pubs and restaurants and, as befits its history as a market town, acts as the obvious place to restock on both essentials and to replace that vital bit of kit you may have broken or left behind at home.

Like an oasis, Banbury exists in virtual isolation, with the area to the South is characterised by a number of small villages some of which offer the opportunity to top up on day-to-day supplies. More importantly, they also act as hosts to a number of good watering holes and places to stay.

SHOPPING

Banbury has put a lot of effort in recent years into raising its attractiveness as a regional shopping centre and it has to a large extent succeeded. The town's modern success is due in no small measure to the substantial Castle Quay development right on the canal in the centre of town which has the usual mix of chain stores and High Street names. To the planners' credit, Castle Quay was developed around a new museum and revamped towpath area and also incorporates Tooley's Boatyard.

Banbury is much more than simply another anonymous mall. It has always been a local market town and signs of this role can be spotted if you wander around what is probably best called now 'the old town', including the white-bricked Lamphrey's Building, an old corn merchant whose bold lettering lists available agricultural supplies. It's also worth just getting lost in the medieval street layout and passing time spotting architectural curiosities.

By concentrating its big name stores in the Castle Quay mall, Banbury has rather cleverly left its High Street to retain a traditional feel, where specialist family-run shops co-exist side by side with the more familiar names. Examples of serendipitous shopping include Hoods the Ironmongers on Bridge Street, a cake decorating shop by the bus station and Fusspots on Parsons Street, a shop dedicated entirely to cooking equipment. Cornhill Books, appropriately enough in Cornhill, also has three storeys of books.

When it comes to supermarkets, Banbury has a large Sainsbury's on the Oxford Road and a Morrison's just off the canal by Bridge 168 on Swan Close Road. There is also a Somerfield inside Castle Quay and a Tesco hidden away in the industrial estate to the north.

Banbury also has a farmers' market on the first Friday of each month and a WI market every Saturday morning (situated at Cornhill). The

Lamb Man (01295 721876) offers farm produced fresh or frozen lamb and Wykham Park Farm Shop (01295 262049) offers home produced beef, fruit and vegetables (asparagus a speciality), free-range eggs and cakes.

Bodicote has a hairdresser and a hat shop, but the nearest source of sustenance is the farm shop near the flyover (01295 270789) alongside the A4260, which offers fruit and vegetables and a range of delicacies, whilst Kings Sutton has a post office in Wales Street and a Co-Op mini-market, as well as a kitchen gadget shop and a hairdresser.

Adderbury has a small post office open Monday afternoons and Friday mornings and 'Taste Buds', a combination of butchers and bakers, although no candlesticks are on offer. This sells fine foods and also acts as the village store.

Deddington can be a good place to pick up supplies; it has two small mini-markets and a post office and holds a farmers' market offering local produce every fourth Saturday in the month. In addition, there is a significant antiques centre and a number of specialist stores, one of which is 'Foodies', a deli and café with a good selection of tempt-

> Modern Banbury cake is a sort of flat Eccles cake with a sugary pastry enclosing mixed fruit, spices and rosewater.

ing fare, including (if you're lucky) Banbury cake. Clifton also has an antiques centre but like Ayhno does not have anywhere to buy more day-to-day necessities.

EATING AND DRINKING

There is no shortage of places to stop for refreshment along this stretch, which includes some of the area's finest restaurants and best pubs. Banbury alone has over sixty pubs and numerous restaurants and rather than list them all, the following far from comprehensive selection is intended as an introduction to some of the more famous, or infamous, amongst them.

BANBURY PUBS

- **The Bell**, 12 Middleton Road (01295 253169) – *a very friendly local with two dining rooms and a heavy sports theme.*
- **The Coach and Horses**, Butchers Row (01295 273552) – *offers live music Friday nights and Sunday lunchtimes.*
- **The Exchange**, 49-50 High Street (01295 259035) – *a large Wetherspoon's pub offering restaurant-style dining.*

- **Ye Olde Reine Deer Inn**, Parsons Street (01295 264031) – *the oldest pub in Banbury and possibly the one with the corniest name!*
- **The Priory**, 38 Bridge Street (01295 270151) – *open 'till the small hours and situated in the centre of town.*
- **The Swan**, South Bar Street (01295 262900) – *live music from 4-7 p.m. on Sundays.*
- **The Wine Vaults**, Parsons Street (01295 273472) – *a family-friendly pub.*

LUNCHES AND LIGHT BITES

- **The Banesberie Coffee Shop,** 10 Butchers Row (01295 269066) – *situated in the middle of town and serving homemade food, with the accent on French and English specialities.*
- **Fillers,** 6 Church Lane (01295 254160) – *sandwiches and snacks.*
- **Geranium Tea Shoppe,** 13 White Lion Walk (01295 257966) – *the extra letters in the word 'Shop' say it all!*
- **The Granary Restaurant,** 6 Butchers Row (01295 250628) – *an accent on salads.*

- **JJ's Bar and Café,** Cornhill.
- **Yogen Fruz,** *a Juice and Shake Bar in the Castle Quay mall.*

Rosamund The Fair is a purpose-built narrowboat restaurant operating out of Tooley's Boatyard. It is available for private hire or public cruises but booking is essential – 01295 278690.

Banbury also has a number of coffee bars and places serving snacks, both in the town centre and within the Castle Quay development.

WESTERN DINING

- **Fabios,** 39 High Street (01295 259636) – *Italian cuisine.*
- **Hyltons,** 27 Parsons Street (01295 270777).
- **Tex's Café,** 56 Bridge Street (01295 264959).

- **Ye Olde Bakehouse,** 48 Parsons Street (01295 262681).

Banbury also has a selection of the usual pizza, chicken and burger houses.

EASTERN DINING

- **Bengal Spice,** 5C George Street (01295 277038) – *Indian restaurant with a takeaway service.*
- **The Forum,** 14 South Bar (01295 276228) – *Chinese restaurant with a takeaway service.*
- **Lin Hong,** 53 High Street (01295 251137) – *Chinese restaurant with a special lunchtime menu.*
- **Mogul Tandoori,** 58 Parsons Street (01295 251920) – *Indian restaurant with a takeaway service.*
- **Sheesh Mahal,** 43 South Bar (01295 266489) – *serves award-*

winning Indian and Pakistani cuisine.
- **Siam House,** 48 Parsons Street (01295 275088) – *Thai restaurant with a takeaway service.*
- **Surma,** 73 Bridge Street (01295 277778) – *Balti and Tandoori.*
- **Thai Orchid,** 56 North Bar, next to St Mary's (01295 270833) – *Lunchtime buffet but book for the evening as it gets very busy despite its extensive size.*
- **Vichi's Restaurant,** 27 Parsons Street (01295 262969) – *more Thai.*

Bodicote has three pubs, which are all quite close together, The Horse and Jockey (no food Sundays and Mondays), the Bakers Arms (closed lunchtimes on Tuesday and Wednesday) and The Plough (01295 262327). The latter looks fairly rustic from the outside but don't let appearances deceive you as the pub is home to its own micro-brewery which produces both Bodicote Bitter, Triple X in winter and 3 Goslings in summer and also serves food. Production from the brewery is sporadic, though.

King's Sutton has one of the easiest pub-crawls in the county, with all three of its pubs within 150yds of each other. The Butchers Arms (01295 810898), a Hook Norton pub, offering traditional English food; The Three Tuns (01295 812685) and the White Horse (01295 810843), a Brakspears pub.

> The 3 Goslings brew is so called because the brewer had three daughters and the pub sits on the side of Goose Lane.

Deddington offers a wide variety of refuelling stops and has no less than four pubs ranging from the Red Lion (01869 338553) on the village square to the Deddington Arms Hotel (01869 338364). The Crown and Tuns (01869 337371) boasts uninterrupted appearances in the *Good Beer Guide* since 1974, while the Unicorn (01869 338838) is an eighteenth-century coaching inn which does both pub food and restaurant meals. The café within 'Foodies' (not open Monday) can be a good place to pause, whilst The Olive Restaurant (01869 338813) next door (also not open Monday) is available if you want something more substantial.

Also in Deddington, Bowlers Brasserie and Restaurant (01869 338813) specialises in game and seafood, while the seventeenth-century Holcombe Hotel (01869 338274) has an award-winning restaurant and also hosts Peppers, where pizza and pasta lead the menu. Alternatively, there's always the May Fu II Chinese restaurant on New Street (01869 338047) if you fancy something more exotic. The Duke of Cumberland's Head in Clifton (01869 338534) is a sixteenth-century thatched inn offering both restaurant meals and bar snacks.

Adderbury itself offers four pubs; The Bell Inn (01295 810338); The Red Lion (01295 810269) on the Oxford Road; The Coach and Horses (01295 810422) and the White Hart (01295 810406). If you're in the mood for something more atmospheric, Adderbury, or more accurately Twyford, also has Le Restaurant Francais at Morgans Orchard (01295 812047), also on the Oxford Road, which is felt by many to be the finest French restaurant for miles around. Just outside Adderbury on the road to Ayhno is The Plough (01295 810327).

The Great Western Arms (01869 338288) on the canal near Ayhno Wharf has recently been renovated and the new owners have created a good combination of traditional pub and a restaurant aimed at the more sophisticated diner. The Cartwright Arms (01869 811111) actually in the village itself also serves good food and even offers to come and fetch you from the towpath if you give them a call.

SLEEPING

There are a wide variety of places to stop over on this stretch, both within Banbury itself and in the villages to the south. Those in Banbury tend to be clustered on the road out to Oxford, for many years the more elegant end of town. The following lists offer a selection of what's available:

HOTELS AND INNS

- **The Banbury House Hotel,** Oxford Road, Banbury (01295 259361) – *Georgian hotel (part of Best Western) with all the usual facilities.*
- **The Bell Inn,** High Street, Adderbury (01295 810338) – *two rooms available at a local village inn.*
- **The Cartwright Arms Hotel,** Aynho (01869 811111) – *sixteenth-century coaching inn with twenty rooms.*
- **Cromwell Lodge Hotel,** 9-11 North Bar Street, Banbury (01295 259781) – *seventeenth-century two star hotel.*
- **The Deddington Arms Hotel,** Horse Fair, Deddington (01869 338364) – *four-posters and family rooms.*
- **The Duke of Cumberland's Head,** Clifton (01869 338643) – *sixteenth-century inn.*
- **Holcombe Hotel,** High Street, Deddington (01869 338274) – *a seventeenth-century quality hotel.*
- **Whatley Hall,** Horsefair, Banbury, next to the cinema, (0870 400 8104) – *a seventeenth-century MacDonald's Hotel with its own resident ghost.*

BED AND BREAKFAST/GUESTHOUSES

- **Amberley Guest House,** Middleton Road, Banbury (01295 255797)
- **Avonlea Guest House,** Southam Road, Banbury (01295 267837)
- **Banbury Cross B&B,** Broughton Road, Banbury (01295 266048) – *Victorian house with car parking.*
- **Calthorpe Lodge Guest House,** Calthorpe Road, Banbury (01295 252325) – *quiet location.*
- **College Farmhouse,** Kings Sutton (01295 811473) – *farmhouse B&B.*
- **Cotefields** (01295 264977) – *B&B attached to a plant nursery.*
- **Easington House,** Oxford Road, Banbury (01295 270181) – *fifteenth-century farmhouse*
- **Fairlawns,** Oxford Road, Banbury (01295 262461) – *family-run Edwardian guesthouse.*
- **Hill Barn,** Milton Gated Road, Deddington (01869 338631) – *farmhouse B&B.*
- **Stonecrop Guesthouse,** Hempton Road, Deddington (01869 338335) – *farmhouse B&B.*
- **Treetops Guest House,** Dashwood Avenue, Banbury (01295 254444) – *small friendly guesthouse.*
- **White Cross House,** Broughton Road, Banbury (01295 277932) – *Victorian home with two rooms.*

CAMPING

There are two campsites along this stretch:

- Bo-Peep campsite and caravan park on **Bo-Peep Farm** (01295 810605) on the Ayhno Road out of Adderbury. *An 8-acre site catering for caravans and canvas.*
- **Twilite Moorings,** Twyford Wharf a mile north-east of Adderbury (01295 812522), *is right on the canal and offers moorings and a caravan park. Phone first about canvas.*

Camping shops along this route include:

- Active Outdoor and Ski, Market Square, Banbury (0800 521171).
- Millets Leisure, 9 High Street, Banbury (01295 263189).
- Outdoor Venture, 22 Castle Quay, Banbury (01295 267785).

SECTION C

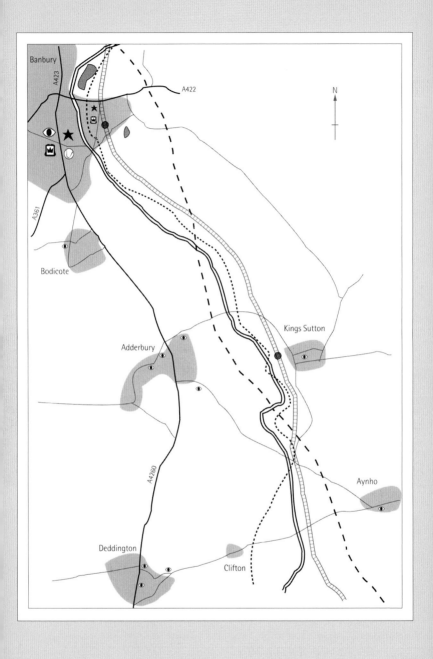

Banbury

A423

A422

N

A361

Bodicote

Kings Sutton

Adderbury

A4260

Aynho

Deddington

Clifton

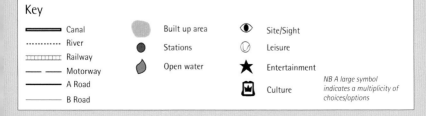

Key

▬▬ Canal		Built up area	◉	Site/Sight
···· River	●	Stations	◎	Leisure
▦▦ Railway	◗	Open water	★	Entertainment
▬ ▬ Motorway			⊞	Culture
▬▬ A Road				
▬ B Road			*NB A large symbol indicates a multiplicity of choices/options*	

SEEING AND DOING

INTRODUCTION

G iven its dominance, it is no surprise that Banbury offers the majority of things to do and see along this stretch, although the local
villages offer some variety. Visiting some of the sites and sights outside
of Banbury gives an insight into the history of the area and how the
relationship between the town and the villages was, and perhaps still is,
a symbiotic one, with each to some extent dependent upon the other.
Whereas Banbury once needed the fruits of the local villagers' labours
to have something to trade, now it needs their disposable income.

SIGHTS

T he first port of call for anyone looking to linger in Banbury should
be the Tourist Information Centre in the Castle Quay Centre (01295
259855). As well as the usual source of leaflets and timings, the centre
also has information on guided walks during the summer months, and
a free leaflet offering a do-it-yourself historic town trail. There are also
similar leaflets covering Bodicote and Deddington, although the latter
is more of a country walk (see 'Sampling').

Banbury's St Mary's church is an unusual late Georgian building
which replaced a mediaeval church, most of which collapsed dramati-
cally one Sunday morning in December 1790, followed shortly by its
tower. Unusually for a church, the building is a perfect square with a
dome supported by twelve classical pillars and a pepper-pot tower. The
design is said to have been based
upon a Wren church. Inside, the
church also has a gallery (which
originally ran along all four sides)
and some richly coloured mosaics.

> In his preface to the 1726 edition of
> *Gulliver's Travels* Jonathan Swift suggests
> that he took the name Gulliver from the
> tombstones at Banbury.

It would be criminal to visit
Banbury and not seek out the famous
Banbury Cross, although the present
edifice to bear the name is not that
attractive to the eye. An example of
Victorian kitsch at its height, it was
erected in 1859 to celebrate the
Queen's daughter's marriage to Prince

> There were originally three crosses, located
> at High Cross, Broad Cross and Market
> Cross, but none of these survived the
> puritanical zeal of the late 1600s, when
> even the local maypole was torn down.

Frederic of Russia. Nooks within the cross were filled in 1914 with images of
Victoria herself, her son King Edward VII and his successor George V, whose
accession to the throne was somewhat belatedly being celebrated.

Tooley's Boatyard (07817 542208) accessed via the towpath or from
the Castle Quay Shopping Centre is a Scheduled Ancient Monument,

SECTION C

largely through its claims to be the country's oldest working dry dock – it has been in continuous use since its opening in 1778.

Until recently however the boatyard looked to the outsider more like a junkyard and its future was in doubt. Luckily Banbury grasped the potential of its canal just in time and it was incorporated into the major re-vamp of the area at the end of the last century. Inevitably perhaps, this was driven by a retail development, but at least this meant that a new home could be found fro the local museum (see below) as well as the boatyard.

These days the dock is encased in a rather grim and functional grey metal, but the walls of the dock itself are glass, allowing passers-by to peep in and watch the craftsmen at work. The boatyard offers guided tours every Friday and Saturday from 2.30 p.m. and has a shop offering both practical chandlery and more popular canalia. For boaters missing a vital piece of kit this is one of the very few chances to access a specialist service on this route, but phoning ahead is advisable. The boatyard is also home to the floating restaurant *Rosamund The Fair* (see 'Basics').

> It was from Banbury in the late 1930s that Tom Rolt set out on his waterways journey on his narrowboat *Cressy*, later chronicled in his book *Narrowboat*, that helped rekindle interest in the inland waterways. On the back of this interest came the Inland Waterways Association who held their second public boat rally here in 1955 to publicise plans to fill the canal in at Banbury. Luckily, their efforts were successful and today Banbury's citizens can put themselves forward as champions of the Oxford Canal rather than the place that nearly did for it!

Half-timbred buildings acting now as shops in Banbury.

Other sights in Banbury's town centre include Lamphrey's Building, the headquarters of an old corn merchandising business which still bears the signs of what it had to offer on the outside, the sixteenth century half timbered façade of 16 Market Place and the spandrels and ironwork ornaments over the entrance to Butchers Row.

Beyond Banbury, if you do the Bodicote Trail (see 'Learn More and Links'), you will pass Upper and Lower Grove Mills, both of which are mentioned in the Domesday Book, as well as Bloxham Grove, a house that dates back to the early eighteenth century at one time owned by George Warriner, a Nottingham linen draper with a business in London's Bond Street – a reminder of Banbury's textile past.

Kings Sutton has a number of curiosities worthy of a village trail but as yet none exists. These include the Bog Spring, which was said to have had great healing properties and almost led to Kings Sutton becoming as famous as Leamington or Bath and St Rumbold's Well, dedicated to St Rumbold who was born in 662 and did well to become beatified as he only lived three days but packed a lot into them: he spoke Holy words, declared himself a Christian and was baptised. There are also some early nineteenth-century stocks where a man was reputedly incarcerated and guarded over by two constables one night in 1858 for being drunk and disorderly.

> The font of the church of St Peter and St Paul is said to be its oldest part and has connections with the remarkable St Rumbold.

Kings Sutton is perhaps most memorable for the 198 foot spire on The church of St Peter and St Paul. Built around 1400 to 1450, this acts as a beacon for all who pass through this stretch.

Deddington is generous with its information boards and the best place to start is the market square, where there a map and summary of the history of the three villages of Deddington, Clifton and Hempton along with the village's recently awarded coat of arms. Deddington never quite made it's preferred status as town, with agriculture the mainstay of the local economy until relatively recently. In 2000 there were still nine working farms here – but together they employed only six people full time.

> The ox on the coat of arms represents Oxfordshire and the horse refers to the village's horse fair. The chained eagle represents Piers Gaveston, who was imprisoned in the castle in 1312.

There isn't a lot left of Deddington Castle on the east side of Deddington, but it is worth a visit if you have a good imagination as extensive earthworks remain, concealing the remains of a twelfth-century edifice, and giving some inkling of how in the past there were some challengers to Banbury's claim to be the major local centre.

Deddington's church has enjoyed a chequered history and can be viewed as a time capsule. Although the basic shape of the church dates back to the fourteenth century, it has been chopped and changed on numerous occasions since to meet the requirements of the religious

SECTION C

leaders and politicians of the day. If you do the Deddington Trail (also available from the Tourist Information Centre) this includes Barford Mill; a listed ironstone corn mill and two nearby two-storey ironstone rubble cottages.

> Deddington's church bells were melted down to make artillery during the Civil War. Although the king promised to replace them, for reasons beyond his control he was unable to honour his pledge and the tower was silent for nearly 150 years.

Adderbury church has a chancel and vestry in the Perpendicular style which were rebuilt between 1408 and 1419, the chief mason being Richard Winchcombe, who also built the Divinity School in Oxford. Along the wall of the north aisle are carved a series of grotesque figures and musicians and their instruments and an eye-catching glass screen. The figures act as corbels and Adderbury is almost unique in having both the quantity and quality of them in its church. It is also worth trying to find the medieval carving of a man blowing a recorder and banging a tambourine on one of the misericords – the wooden tip up seats in the choir stalls. Behind Adderbury House lie Adderbury Lakes, a nature reserve run by the county council.

St Michael and All Angels at **Ayhno** is built of Limestone and dates back to the fourteenth century. The church never really recovered from damage inflicted during the civil war and it was partially demolished in 1723 and rebuilt in the Grecian style. Just outside the church you can see the old preaching cross. From the churchyard look over into the grounds

> Ice hacked out of the canal could keep for two years when packed in straw in the icehouse at Aynhoe Park.

of Aynhoe Park and you might just make out an old icehouse. This was used to store ice in the days before refrigeration. The house itself is open on Wednesday and Thursday afternoons May to September (01869 810636).

CULTURE

There is one cinema along this stretch, and not surprisingly it is in Banbury (01295 278212). This is an Odeon and lies to the west of the town, whereas most of the other cultural highlights cluster around the redevelopment to the east.

Banbury Museum (01295 259855), situated within the Castle Quay Shopping Centre, has won awards for its architecture and could yet win some for its displays. Entrance is free and the main galleries are sited on the opposite side of the canal from the shops, but these are reached via a glass walkway over the water, which appropriately enough houses a series of waterways discovery exhibits. These are complemented by short videos setting out some of the history of the canal and Banbury's special role in that history.

Boats passing by Ayhno Weir.

The main galleries have plenty of hands-on exhibits for children and the simply curious-minded. Highlights include a Civil War cannon found buried in the remains of the castle in 1974 and the cross bar of the gibbet from which convicted felons were hanged and left to rot right into the eighteenth century. By a quirk of fate, the beam survived because it was employed as part of a plush loom.

The Mill Arts Centre (01295 252050) adjacent to the canal acts as a venue for several resident companies and the Creative Arts Network, which brings together like-minded artists and craftspeople every fourth Wednesday. The Mill is also home to the Millstream Café Bar, which is open over lunchtimes and in the evenings Tuesday to Saturday.

Kings Sutton has been known to hold its own Literary Festival and Aynho has its very own Ayhno Community Theatre (01869 811178), a village amateur dramatic group which aims to put on three productions a year in the village hall or occasionally outdoors.

ENTERTAINMENT

- **The Ride a Cock Horse Folk Club** – *every Wednesday at 8:30 p.m. in the Millers Bar in The Mill, Spiceball Park, Banbury.*
- **Livearts at St Mary's** – *an arts venue based in St Mary's church on Horsefair in Banbury* (01295 253329). *There's a constantly changing programme of events, so it's wise to phone on ahead to see what's on.*
- **The Spiceball Park Sports Centre** on Spiceball Park Road in Banbury (01295 257522) – *a 25m swimming pool and trainer pool as well as squash courts, a sports hall, a workout studio/gym and even a fast tanning sunbed if the weather is letting you down.*
- **Woodgreeen Leisure Centre** (01295 262742) *is off Orchard Way also in Banbury and boasts a 50m outdoor Olympic swimming pool and an international indoor bowls rink.*

NIGHT CLUBS
- **52° North**, South Bar Street (01295 259933).
- **Hobson's Choice**, 5 Butchers Row (01295 262611).
- **The Sound Exchange**, 449-50 High Street (01295 275057).

SECTION C

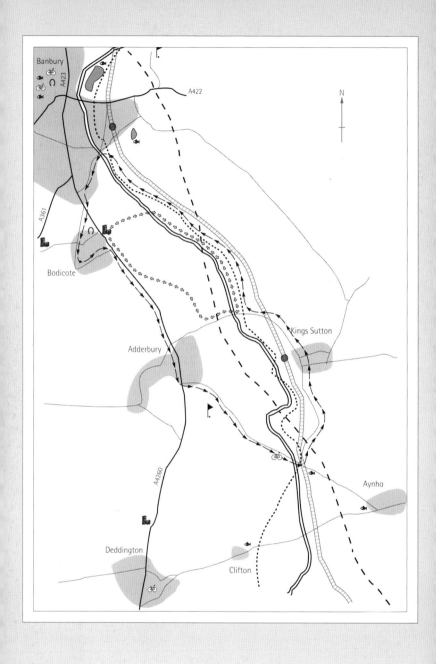

Banbury

A422

A423

A361

N

Bodicote

Adderbury

Kings Sutton

A4260

Aynho

Deddington

Clifton

Key

▬▬▬ Canal	Built up area	Cycling route/outlet	Riding outlet
········· River	Stations	Walking route/outlet	Golf course/outlet
▦▦▦ Railway	Open water	Fishing spot/outlet	
▬ ▬ Motorway			
▬▬ A Road			
▬▬ B Road			

SAMPLING

INTRODUCTION

This stretch offers plenty of opportunities for sampling the local landscape, although the canal tends to follow the valley of the River Cherwell and as such there can be steep hills either side of the towpath. The spread of local villages, combined with the proximity of Banbury, mean that the area is well served with both major and minor roads, making it easy to get around. The presence of the Cherwell also adds another dimension in terms of history as well as flora and wildlife, as well as opportunities for fishing.

The OS Explorer Map covering this stretch is number 191, Banbury, Bicester and Chipping Norton.

WALKING

The towpath represents the main walking thoroughfare through this stretch, although there is the usual pattern of footpaths across cutting across fields. Generally, these are well maintained, although some have been moved in recent years to accommodate the M40. Public footpaths along this stretch tend to follow a north–south trajectory rather than east–west, with the river acting as more of a natural obstacle than the canal. Care should therefore be taken in planning circular walks.

Walk C starts to the east of Bodicote just off the Oxford Road and runs alongside the canal for 1.5 miles before cutting across fields to rejoin the road. The walk allows a perfect opportunity to sample both the local countryside and to take in an expansive view of the Cherwell Valley, incorporating in turn the canal, the railway and the motorway, and how they have all selected to follow essentially the same route as they pass through this part of north Oxfordshire.

The ancient Salt Way cuts through Bodicote to the north of the stretch and can be enjoyed through a 2-mile nature trail, details of which are available from the Tourist Information Centre in Banbury (see 'Learn More and Links'). The path is prehistoric in origin and is thought to have linked Droitwich in the Midlands, which is famous for its salt, with London. These days much of the route follows modern roads but it retains its country lane route through Bodicote. The Tourist Information Centre can also provide leaflets of walks through Deddington and an historic town trail through Banbury.

> Until 100 years ago a May Day ceremony took place on the Salt Way where the sunrise was greeted by the blowing of horns.

SECTION C

Also worthy of note on this stretch is Daeda's Wood, owned by the Woodland Trust but bought on behalf of the villagers of Deddington after a period of fund raising that took only four weeks. The wood contains 4 hectares (10 acres) of oak, ash, willow and alder, a total of 3,700 trees and shrubs on the banks of the River Swere, where there is a bench overlooking the water. The wood also has circular paths round it and there are regular talks by local enthusiasts about the wood and the wildlife within it. Also, don't forget Adderbury Lakes.

SECTION C

SECTION C WALK

To Bodicote and Back

Description:	*A gentle stroll with some slight hills offering a good view over Banbury in its early stages.*
Distance:	*3.75 miles*
Duration:	*1.25–1.5 hrs*
Staring point:	*Grid Reference 465381, OS Explorer 191*
Nearest Refreshment:	*The Plough in Bodicote.*

Start from the service road alongside some houses and take the track heading left, called appropriately enough Canal Lane. Follow this half made up farm road and public bridleway for about a mile downhill across open fields until you reach a renovated bridge over the canal. Go over this and follow the towpath to your right.

Pass under the motorway and then under the picturesque picket fenced Bridge 174 at Grants Lock. Leave the canal at Twyford Wharf (Bridge 177) and cross over the bridge and up the hill to your right. Immediately after crossing the top of the motorway take the public footpath to the right indicating Bodicote as 1.25 miles away.

Cross a series of stiles and turn half left over a field when you reach a dip, heading for the left-hand side of the barn. Go through the gate at the breast of the hill and follow the path back to the road, passing an impressive rugby ground on your left. On reaching the road cross over and turn right along the pavement and head back to the starting point.

Outlets selling walking equipment supplies along this stretch include Millets, High Street, Banbury (01295 263189).

CYCLING

The canal towpath also acts as a natural focus for many circular cycle routes, although it can get a bit bumpy in sections between Grants Lock and Ayhno Weir. Easy access to the towpath can be gained from Banbury as well as at Twyford Wharf, Nell Bridge and Ayhno Wharf. Each of these has somewhere to park.

Oxfordshire County Council also produces a leaflet describing a 25-mile ride on mainly metalled roads to the west of Banbury called the Ironstone Villages Bicycle Ride, which starts and finishes in Bodicote. Copies are available at Banbury Tourist Information Centre.

One suggested ride (around 12 miles in total) starts at Kings Sutton, where there's a railway station as well as plenty of street-side parking. Start by taking the Banbury Lane north, swooping downhill to join Twyford Wharf and the canal. From here head north into Banbury beside the water and then head back down south using minor roads around the edge of Banbury and through Bodicote before being forced to use the busy Oxford Road for a couple of miles into Adderbury. A left turn here takes you towards Aynho, with a right before the village returning you into Kings Sutton. Don't be tempted to rejoin the towpath at Nell's Bridge though as the going can get rough here and there's no obvious route off the towpath back to your starting point with both the Cherwell and the railway line forming natural barriers.

Bike shops along this stretch include:

- **Banbury Cycles**, 55 Broad Street, Banbury (01295 259349).
- **BGM**, 2 Bridge Street, Banbury (01295 272757).
- **Cyclogical**, Hudson Street, Deddington (01869 338090).

RIDING

Public bridleways along this stretch include the Jurassic Way heading out of Bodicote to the north-east, and along the Salt Way, to the north-west of Bodicote, with the latter incorporating a junction with another bridleway heading due south towards Milton, west of Adderbury. There is also a bridleway heading east away from Twyford Mill and another linking Kings Sutton with the B4100 just west of Aynho.

Slightly out of the area, Gentle Giants at Tarmarton (01295 780700) offer the opportunity to hire a Shire team and driver for the day.

Equestrian suppliers along this stretch include:

- **Banbury Cross Farm Supplies Ltd**, 19 West Bar, Banbury (01295 267744).
- **Bodicote Flyover Farm Shop**, Bodicote (01295 270789).

SECTION C

FISHING

Most of the fishing on this stretch, certainly that covering the canal and the River Cherwell, comes under the jurisdiction of either the Banbury and District Angling Association (01295 268047), or the Coventry and District AA (024 7626 9502).

The stretch north of Banbury to Hardwick Lock is reckoned to be particularly bountiful, with large carp, roach of up to a pound and chub and bream up to 3lb. Elsewhere on the canal there is the usual mix of roach, bream, perch and pike, with carp supposedly up to 20lb in places. In addition, the association can arrange day tickets for the following:

- **Banbury Reservoir**
- **Spital Farm Lake**, Grimsbury
- **Slinkit Lake**, Ayhno

Other local fishing spots include:

- **College Farm Fishing**, Ayhno (01869 810258) – *lake with Mirror and Crucian Carp, Chub, Bream, Roach, Rudd and Tench.*
- **The Goldfish Bowl**, Clifton (01869 338539) – *lake with Golden, Mirror and Common Carp.*
- **Nell Bridge Coarse Fishery**, Ayhno (01295 811227) – *three lakes (including Slinket Lake) with Tench, Roach, Rudd, Perch, Mirror, Common Carp and Bream.*

Fishing shops along this stretch include:

- **Banbury Gunsmiths and Fishing Tackle**, 47a Broad Street, Banbury (01295 265819).
- **Castaway**, 88 Warwick Road, Banbury (01295 254274).

OTHER

There are two golf courses along this stretch:

- **Cherwell Edge Golf Club**, Chacombe near Banbury (01295 711591) – *18 holes, 5,947yds. Also includes a floodlit driving range and putting green as well as a pro shop.*
- **Banbury Golf Centre**, Ayhno Road, Adderbury (01295 810419) – *23 holes, 6,365yds. Also includes a putting green.*

SECTION D

AYHNO TO GIBRALTAR

94

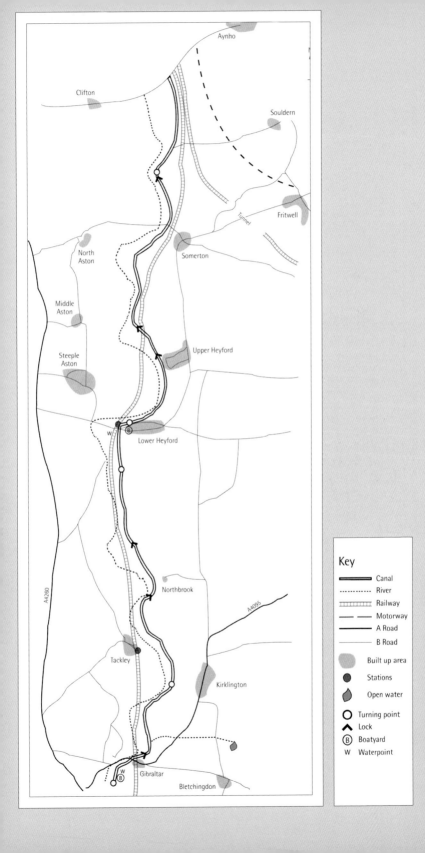

Key

▬▬▬▬	Canal
··········	River
▥▥▥▥	Railway
— — —	Motorway
▬▬▬	A Road
———	B Road
🟫	Built up area
🔴	Stations
🟤	Open water
○	Turning point
⌃	Lock
Ⓑ	Boatyard
W	Waterpoint

Aynho

Clifton

Souldern

Tunnel

Fritwell

North Aston

Somerton

Middle Aston

Steeple Aston

Upper Heyford

W Ⓑ

Lower Heyford

A4260

Northbrook

A4095

Tackley

Kirklington

W
Ⓑ

Gibraltar

Bletchingdon

SHAPERS

THE CANAL ON THIS STRETCH

KEY FACTS

LENGTH: 11 miles

BOATYARDS: 2
  Lower Heyford
  Enslow Mill Wharf

WATERPOINTS: 2
  Lower Heyford
  Enslow

TURNING POINTS: 5
  Somerton
  Lower Heyford Wharf
  Lower Heyford
  Kirtlington
  Enslow

LOCKS: 6
  Somerton Deep Lock (12ft 0in)
  Heyford Common Lock (7ft 2in)
  Allen's Lock (5ft 0in)
  Dashwood Lock (9ft 3in)
  Northbrook Lock (5ft 0in)
  Pigeon's Lock (8ft 4in)

Railway, river and canal run alongside each other through most of this section, coming teasingly close on a number of occasions before pulling apart. The railway eventually comes as near as it dares at Heyford, whilst the section ends with the Cherwell and canal actually becoming one for a short distance, with delightful results.

After leaving Ayhno Wharf the canal is sandwiched between the flat flood plain of the River Cherwell to the west and railway lines to the east, with the latter imposing their presence early on with an impressive viaduct. A landscape of lush fields soon becomes a hallmark of this stretch, with the widespread flooding the Cherwell is prone to a possible explanation.

During the winter months the meadows hereabouts can resemble a lake and it is not totally unknown for sections of the canal to get swallowed up in the deluge. Generally, however, the waterway is protected by an embankment, which provides both protection and a viewing platform.

One long straight section follows Bridge 192 and Wharf Farm, followed by another with good moorings, a characteristic of this section through to Somerton. The towpath is also pretty solid and popular with walkers and cyclists alike. After the lift bridge (Number 193) a short stretch follows that curves languidly to the left before Somerton Deep Lock.

A footpath off to the right the other side of Heyford's Lift Bridge takes the walker over a pair of bridges and through an area of environmentally sensitive wetlands characterised by hay meadows and wet pastures which support both wild flowers and rare breeding birds.

Just before the lock there is a winding hole (60ft max) where the Cherwell kisses the towpath briefly like a chaste lover before scurrying away to the west where its path can be traced by a line of willows. Somerton Deep Lock is aptly named as its 12ft drop can take some time to negotiate. The good folk at the lock house keep an immaculate garden and offer a selection of second-hand books and ice creams – just ring the bell to get their attention.

Look out for a series of wooden sculptures by Michael Fairfax, made from old lock timbers. They are inscribed with a poem called, appropriately enough, 'Lock' by Jamie McKendrick.

The bank is less conducive to mooring the other side of the lock but the towpath remains solid through to Somerton itself which lies half a mile to the east of Bridge 196, its church spire clearly visible on a hill above. On reaching the bridge it's the railway's turn to come alongside where a sign tells passengers the name of the waterway they're gazing down on.

There's another winding hole (max. 56ft) the other side of the bridge and a large meadow on the towpath side. Mooring is possible just past the abandoned bridge but after this the bank becomes dis-

The Causeway by Bridge 199 was originally made just wide enough to take a horse and cart but suffered during the war when it was used by tanks to cross the Cherwell meadow.

tinctly less friendly, disappearing for a brief while as the canal dips into a rare cutting lined with trees, after which it reasserts its open nature all the way through to Heyford Common Lock.

The influence of the Cherwell and presence of the railway remain very much in evidence along this stretch, with pollarded willows a regular feature. The two combine to sandwich the canal by Bridge 199, with the river becoming more daring in its approaches pending full consumation on reaching Heyford. Middle and Steeple Aston lie to the west, and the steeple of Upper Heyford's church soon rises up in the east. Just before Heyford Common Lock the bank becomes reinforced once again and the lock itself manifests just after a steep bend to the left.

After the lock the railway crosses over the water and the houses of the larger of the two Heyfords (the Lower), become visible straight ahead after Bridge 202. The arrival of civilisation comes as something of a surprise after a long period of apparent isolation. Before this however there is Allen's Lock, with the Cherwell now running alongside the canal, with Bridge 204 (Allen's Bridge) a popular access point for those wishing to use the towpath, partly due to the parking offered there. From here the towpath is very even and offers a pleasantly wooded, if deceptively long, path into Heyford.

Upper Heyford is inaccessible from the towpath, but the steep bank leading up to the church offers an impressive aspect, with a long stone barn suggesting faded grandeur. The approach to Lower Heyford is along the back of some impressive houses and ends with an awkward lift bridge.

Back by the canal the towpath leads along the northern limit of the village, which can be accessed either by the lift bridge or at Heyford Wharf. A tree house hangs precariously over the water and the towpath is usually lined with both long-term and visitor moorings (14 day and 48 hour).

Heyford Wharf marina (01869 340348) is a base for hire boats and has a winding hole (70ft) dating back to its days as a coal wharf. The yard offers a good range of services and a small shop, but can be busy on 'turnaround' days. The popularity of this spot may also be in part due to its position alongside one of the railway stations on this section. There's a water point just south of Bridge 206 and another 70ft winding hole amongst the trees just beyond the next bridge, where the Cherwell makes yet another appearance.

A hedge lines the path after Dashwood Lock and Bridge, with occasional gaps allowing views of open fields to the right. This gives way to trees as the Cherwell comes alongside once more at Northbrook Lock. Mooring can be fairly tricky along this stretch due to reeds and shallow water and the towpath cuts through woods. Picnic facilities on the non-towpath side at the base of Kirtlington Quarry can be accessed by boat, with mooring permissible for 24 hours.

The picturesque Pigeon's Lock soon follows, where there is road access via a bumpy track, followed by a long straight leading to a wide sweeping bend that brings you to the woods at Enslow Wharf and another turning point and some basic boating supplies. Just before the canalside Rock of Gibraltar pub

> Appropriately, given its name, the Rock of Gibraltar was once the site of a wharf for a significant quarrying business.

look out for the wharfside house with its patio doors opening straight out onto the water. Just the other side of the bridge there's a long line of moored boats leading to Blake's Lock, where the Cherwell and canal finally come together.

PRINCIPAL TOWNS AND VILLAGES
ON THIS STRETCH

BLETCHINGDON
A typical Cotswold village in two parts, linked by footpath and road, with St Giles church and some rather exclusive residences tucked away in the appropriately named Church End, and the heart of the village complete with green, shop, school and pub at the other. Between them,

like the meat in a sandwich, is Bletchingdon Park, whose fine house can just be seen behind the hedges that line the footpath.

FRITWELL

A deceptively large village with a school in the centre. The village still exhibits its farming roots and has an impressive memorial lychgate at the entrance to the church.

GIBRALTAR

Originally a significant canal-side wharf, this small settlement is now principally a collection of commercial units and a pub with one or two cottages. The fact that Gibraltar is passed by rather than through is signified by the modern functional bridge that has usurped the older road bridge that still stands.

KIRTLINGTON

A straggling village nestling between a golf club and a polo ground. There are two village greens, one has the regulation pond whilst the church, pubs and shop congregate near the other. The village has a range of building styles ranging from traditional thatch through honey-coloured Cotswold stone to Georgian.

LOWER HEYFORD

A pretty canal-side village which has benefited from being tucked away behind the main road. Stone cottages predominate, some of which are thatched, with a vibrant pub at one end of the intriguingly named Freehold Street, and outside what used to be the market square, providing a focal point.

> The Heyfords are said to get their name from the discovery by early tribesmen that it was possible to pass through the river here, giving them the name 'Hegford' or high ford. The discovery of a second ford further down led to the division into Upper and Lower Heyford.

MIDDLE ASTON

A small village with much recent building, not all of it sympathetic to the prevalent Cotswold stone theme.

NORTH ASTON

A hamlet clustered around a village green. The church and manor house both lie to the east where the village originally stood.

ROUSHAM

A single street hamlet that backs onto the Cherwell dominated by Rousham House.

SOMERTON

A largely linear village of stone and tile cottages sitting on the side of a hill at the base of which lies the railway, the Cherwell and the canal.

SOULDERN

A sleepy village with no apparent natural focus, although there is a small pond off the main street. As if to emphasise the dispersed nature of the village the church is tucked away down a small lane.

STEEPLE ASTON

A pretty village sitting either side of a dip with over thirty Grade II listed buildings and a shop, as well as an interesting church.

TACKLEY

A deceptively spread-out place with clear 'old' and 'new' ends. The former has both the church and Tackley

The name Aston means 'east' and these three villages mark the limit of early settlement with the river and marshland forming a natural barrier.

Park guarding one entrance to the village, whilst the latter holds the more modern heart with all the main services excluding the pub, which sits between the two near the pretty village green. Tackley is also significant for having one of the two railway stations along this stretch.

UPPER HEYFORD

A curate's egg of a village, with pretty thatched cottages complete with climbing roses juxtaposed with more modern utilitarian housing, the whole sitting on a hillside leading down to the church.

HISTORY

The Cherwell, along with the later growth of Oxford, has been one of the defining historical shapers for settlement in this area. Trade routes and geographical chance combined with access to the water to create natural gathering points from which hamlets and, in time, more sustainable communities developed. For a long time much of the area covered by this section was a large 'no-go' area dividing rival Saxon tribes, stifling settlement. The Cherwell also acted as both a practical and a psychological barrier.

A good example of the influence of traditional routes is Souldern which although unprepossessing now was once at the confluence of two Roman roads, a strategic position that led in time to gradual settlement. After the Norman Conquest, Souldern was large enough to be bestowed to Jordan de Sai, who built a church and became its patron. Equally, Fritwell was adjacent to the Roman Portway and was near the Wattlebank, one of the Britons' lines of defence against the Saxons.

In the Middle Ages Fritwell was the location of the Hundred Moot, where people would gather every month to try disputes. By the mid-nineteenth century, however, its only contact with the outside world was a postman who came from 6 miles away by donkey.

It is no surprise that, given the vantage point it offers, the hill the Astons sit on became an early point of settlement. The Cherwell in the valley below marked a clear boundary and a good 'neutral spot' to gather to parlay or trade. This place was marked with a wooden or stone pillar, known in Saxon as a 'Stapol', and it is from this rather than the church that Steeple Aston gets its name.

Once settlement did take root the fortunes of the different hamlets and villages varied. One good example is Caulcott to the east of Lower

SECTION D

Heyford. At one point this was a much more significant centre than its neighbour, but today it is little more than a collection of farms off a 'B' road.

After the Conquest the feudal system meant that the constant threat of random attack from neighbouring tribes subsided and farming became the natural economic activity for those living in these scattered villages, with the Cherwell providing an additional source of income in the form of fishponds and milling. Despite this, life remained hard and prosperity rose and fell with nature's cycles. This fragility was exposed by the Black Death, which led to many local settlements being abandoned.

Man also had an influence, with the Church and their monasteries wielding considerable power over those tilling the soil, at times almost taxing them out of existence, and for centuries life in this part of the world was a long (or just as often short) struggle for survival. Souldern again provides a good example, with Jordan de Sai giving away the church he had founded to Eynsham Abbey when his son William died, a decision which led to five centuries of service during which the village effectively existed to enrich the monastery's coffers.

Over time the growth of Oxford began to have an impact on the relative economic prosperity of the local villages, both in terms of the power of its colleges and the more day-to-day need to supply the people who lived there with food and the industry that constituted the 'town' side of the 'town and gown' divide with raw materials.

To encourage sales of wool, the Woollen Act decreed that the dead should be wrapped in wool and put in coffins lined with wool. Although largely ignored by the end of the eighteenth century, the Act was not repealed until 1815.

From around the seventeenth century onwards the grazing of sheep and cattle, as well as arable farming, brought a level of prosperity to the local villages that few had ever experienced before. During this time the Cherwell provided the power for a series of mills as well as a medium for raising fish and eels to supply markets in Oxford.

For some this was to be a brief respite however as the Civil War, and the proximity of King Charles, who had made Oxford his capital, unsettled the emerging order. During this time the woodlands to the east of the Heyfords were raided for fuel and building materials by soldiers from both sides to such an extent that they never really recovered.

Luckily, one Royalist scheme that would have had the effect of severing the already fragile communications network linking the villages along this stretch was never put into effect. This was a plan to demolish all the bridges, mills and weirs from the Cherwell to provide an alternative to the Thames for supplying the King's men in Oxford.

During this period, many families were forced to make a difficult choice, often balancing their conscience with more practical considerations. The consequence for those who chose the losing side was often devastating both personally and for the villages they owned once the war finally ended. Sir Thomas Coghill, owner of Bletchingdon House, ended up placing himself in debtor's prison in order to put a stop to the drain on his fortune presented by Cromwell's constant heavy fines.

The growth of Oxford as a place of learning, and in particular the emphasis on the college system, also impacted upon the local area. As early as the fourteenth century the Upper Heyford estate was given to New College by William of Wykeham, who had bought up a number of manors following the collapse in land values after the Black Death. Equally, Lower Heyford later became the property of Corpus Christi College, who bought it for a little over £700.

Later on the Enclosures also had a profound impact. As the power of the monasteries faded, and in time that of the feudal system too, free men had found ways of owning their own land but landlords, many of whom did not even live near their land, discovered that by enclosing their land they could earn much more from it. The strips used by labourers to supplement their income and their diet disappeared. Soon large houses rose to take their place, built using the extra income Enclosure had generated, and although many have since fallen into decay a good number are still dotted about the local landscape.

The fate of Middle Aston provides a good illustration of what could happen during this period. The estate was owned by the much hated Francis Page, politician and 'hanging judge', who then did a deal with the local rector to acquire land previously held by the Church. Having got his hands on the entirety Page enclosed the land and went on to impose his unlikeable personality on the village, going so far as to effectively sequester the church in Steeple Aston and reshape it to meet his whims.

Much later on, in the mid-nineteenth century, Upper Heyford also suffered, as local landowners including New College and the Earl of Jersey secured the required Act of Parliament. Immediately the Roman road through the parish disappeared, along with Cow Common, where the locals grazed their cattle. All they got in return was a small parcel of land for 'exercise and recreation'. The same fate befell their near neighbours in Lower Heyford, who in return for losing 1,700 acres of open fields received the rent from only 32 acres as payment for the poor, distributed as coal at Christmas.

Throughout the centuries communications between the local villages and to the wider world acted as a significant brake on local development, with the villages functioning largely as discrete communities, with the Cherwell still acting as a barrier.

Ironically, it was a waterway that changed all this towards the end of the eighteenth century, when the Oxford Canal offered a link to the unknown lands to the north. Although King Charles' scheme to make the Cherwell navigable had failed, large sections of it had been used to transport goods on a modest scale, notably by Sanderson Miller, a merchant from Banbury who used flat-bottomed boats to take goods upstream, and it was from Banbury that the new waterway also came.

The canal was reliable and able to take significant loads. In the early days the most important cargo was coal, and when the canal finally opened all the way to Oxford the event was celebrated with a flotilla carrying over 200 tons of the black stuff – an unimaginable amount.

Despite the undoubted benefits it brought not everyone welcomed the canal. Its building led to the demolition of the ford, mill and old road to the mill in Upper Heyford and, at the Church's insistence, the waterway was closed on Sundays. Progress was irresistible however and access to the world beyond was expanded further with the coming of the railway, which in time allowed people to commute outside of their immediate community for work and pleasure, a process made all the more complete when the line was extended out from Banbury towards Birmingham. Today, two stations remain on this section, at Tackley and Lower Heyford, the station at Bletchingdon having been a victim of the Beeching cuts in the 1960s.

THE NATURAL LANDSCAPE

From Somerton the River Cherwell starts on its descent into the steepest portion of the valley, and this is also something of a watershed with one stream heading downhill into the Cherwell whilst another heads out west towards the Ouse. Beyond this large expanse the three Astons sit on a set of hills regarded as the furthest ridge of the Outer Cotswolds. These subside to form flatter ground that hosts both Rousham Park and Tackley Woods before rising slightly again.

On the opposite side of the canal the defining feature of the landscape are the flatlands to the east of the Heyfords whose natural features were exploited in the creation of Upper Heyford airfield. Below this the land gives way to a series of scattered woods, coverts and spinneys all the way down to Bletchingdon, which seem to thrive on the local limestone and clays. These sit on wide flat plains largely devoid of settlement until Kirtlington is reached.

At Kirtlington there is a disused quarry once owned by Blue Circle Cement. It is now a nature reserve offering a good spot to understand the underlying geology of the area, with exposed limestone, marls and clays. The quarry is also famed for its dinosaur remains. If all of this summons up visions of despoliation, the perfection of the golf course just to the south of the quarry presents a much calmer vista.

Although there is the occasional stream along this stretch, notably the one that divides Steeple Aston, water tends to be concentrated in the river and the canal, although there is a smattering of manmade lakes associated with the various large houses linked to the villages hereabouts.

ACCESS AND TRANSPORT

ROADS

The A4260 traces a line to the west of the canal for most of this stretch from North Aston to points south, with the A4095 the only other 'A' road making an appearance, rising from the south and passing through

Kirtlington before heading east. About halfway through the section the B4030 bypasses Lower Heyford (and a little further to the east is known as the Lower Heyford Road) and links up with the A4260 at 'Hopcroft's Holt', now the site of a pub indicating its significance as a major junction for some centuries. Otherwise, this section is a series of minor roads.

RAIL
This section has the luxury of two railway stations, at Lower Heyford and Tackley – both on the same line – run by Thames Trains (part of First Great Western) out of Oxford. National Train Enquiries can be reached on 08457 484950.

BUSES
This section is served by a handful of bus services, with local groups in some cases having taken matters into their own hands to improve access to public transport. The most significant companies providing services are:

- **Cherwell Villager** (01295 273086)
  The 51, a circular service linking Banbury with North Aston, Somerton, Souldern and Fritwell (Mondays only).
  The 57, a Banbury circular route operating on Saturdays, taking in North Aston.
- **Heyfordian Travel** (01869 241500)
  The 81 linking Bicester and Banbury Mondays to Saturdays, taking in Somerton and Souldern.
  The 82 linking Lower Heyford and Steeple Aston with Bicester on Fridays only.
  The 90, running on Thursday and Saturday, taking in North Aston.
- **Kidlington Lnyx** (01865 374442)
  A community bus service run by volunteers providing Route 2, *a circular run starting and ending in Kidlington and taking in Kirtlington on Mondays;* Route 3 *linking Kidlington with Bicester on Tuesdays*

taking in Steeple Aston, Souldern and the Heyfords and **Route 4** *again linking Kidlington and Bicester but via Bletchingdon on Thursdays.*
- **North Aston Minibus** (01869 347252)
  A minibus taking elderly North Aston residents into Banbury on the last Thursday of every month at no charge.
- **Stagecoach Oxford** (01865 772250)
  The 25 and 25a linking Bicester and Oxford, taking in the Heyfords, Kirtlington and Blechingdon at roughly hourly intervals Mondays to Saturdays.
  The X59 linking Oxford and Banbury but taking in Tackley and Souldern along the way (Mon-Sat)

Traveline (www.traveline.org.uk) on 0870 6082608 can give details of specific services between 7 a.m. and 10 p.m.

TAXIS
Taxi companies serving this area include **VA and TM Page Taxis**, Upper Heyford (01869 232302). Otherwise, consult Section C for companies running out of Banbury or Section E for companies running out of Oxford.

SECTION D

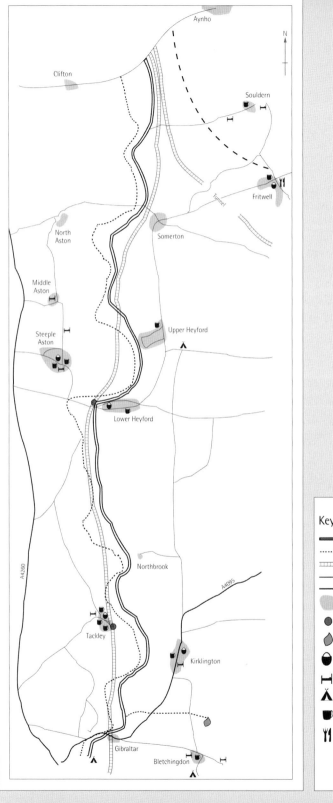

N

Aynho

Clifton

Souldern

⊢⊣

Fritwell

⊢⊣ ̈⟨¶

Tunnel

North
Aston

Somerton

Middle
Aston
⊢⊣

Steeple
Aston
⊢⊣

Upper Heyford

⋀

Lower Heyford

Northbrook

A4260

A4095

Tackley
⊢⊣

Kirklington

Gibraltar
⋀

Bletchingdon
⊢⊣
⋀

Key

▬▬▬	Canal
········	River
▥▥▥	Railway
─ ─ ─	Motorway
─────	A Road
▨	Built up area
●	Stations
⬤	Open water
◗	Shops
⊢⊣	Accomodation
⋀	Campsite
☕	Pub
¶	Restaurant

BASICS

INTRODUCTION

In shopping terms the post-Banbury doldrums that began in the previous section continue along this stretch, although opportunities to stock up on basics do exist. The villages covered here offer a good selection of village pubs, although the precarious nature of the trade these days is illustrated by the number that have closed in recent years and if you are relying on a particular hostelry being open it may be worth phoning on ahead first.

On a more positive note, the villages covered in this section seem to benefit from a geographical location that is near to Oxford, but far enough away to offer easy access to other local attractions whilst still being firmly in the countryside. This advantage is particularly apparent in the number of possible places to stay, ranging from hotels to campsites, taking in a few local B&Bs along the way.

SHOPPING

A recurring feature of the villages along this stretch is the number of village stores that have realised that their future lies in becoming a focal point for their local community. This may seem obvious, but it is a lesson all too many such stores failed to learn during the last two decades of the last century, leading ultimately to their closure and another nail in the coffin of community spirit.

Typically, a local post office lies at the hub of these stores, but is but one of many services on offer. Alongside the traditional standbys of groceries and newspapers these stores have branched out into services such as dry cleaning collection, electronic mobile phone top-ups, photocopying and ATMs.

Many have also understood the importance of creating a more symbiotic relationship with other local businesses and focus on the provision of locally grown or made goods and produce. These stores are mini-case studies of entrepreneurialism advertising themselves on the internet (some even offer access to the web) and meeting perceived gaps in local needs.

One of the best examples of these stores is Wrightons in Fritwell, which shares its premises with a local butcher (01869 345229) and offers the usual selection of groceries and post office as well as added extras such as a free book swap service, home-baked crusty loaves, and an ATM.

Harris's Stores on the corner at the top of the hill in Steeple Aston is another, with an ATM, post office, newsagent and local fruit and vegetables as well as an off-licence and plants. A feature of this store is its long opening hours (8 a.m.-7 p.m.).

Lower Heyford.   *Upper Heyford.*

The Wharf Shop at Lower Heyford Marina was until recently a modest affair catering mostly to boaters, but more recently it has taken to styling itself the village shop in the absence of any competition for the title. Fresh shelving has allowed it to extend its range of dry food and milk. Although it has yet to be seen how successful this experiment will be everyone with an interest in local communities should wish it luck.

The village stores in Tackley have gone one step further than most and actually housed themselves in the village hall, which is also sited conveniently for the local primary school and playing fields. The stores offer the usual range of goods and services and it's worth a rummage in their chilled cabinets to seek out specialist local produce.

The Kirtlington Stores are located just next to the Oxford Arms and are deceptively large, extending out to a conservatory offering hand made greetings cards at the back. Similarly, as well as a post office, the shop on the Green, Bletchingdon, offers a range of basic foods and an off-licence.

EATING AND DRINKING

SECTION D

In the courtyards of a number of the pubs along this stretch you may spot a large canvas sheet with a large circle painted on it, with a stubbly wooden block stuck on a metal stake in front of it. This is the game of Aunt Sally, a pub pastime unique to the Oxfordshire area, which was supposedly introduced by Royalist soldiers during the Civil War.

In the game, players 10yds away throw 18in long skittles at the wooden block, the 'Dolly', which rests on the 'Iron' 2.5ft above

> An alternative theory on the origin of Aunt Sally suggests that it derives from a blood sport known as 'throwing at cocks'. In this game a cock was tied by one leg to a stake and players would take turns throwing clubs at it. The player who killed the bird got to keep it for his pot.

ground level. Each turn involves six throws and a hit is recorded if the stick hits the Dolly before the Iron. Each team consists of eight players and three legs or 'horses' are played, during which each member of the team gets to throw once, making a maximum total of forty-eight hits (the record is thought to stand at forty).

There is a good selection of village pubs along this stretch, many of which participate in Aunt Sally Leagues. Other than the hotels mentioned below these are probably your best bet for food locally, although again it's probably advisable to phone on ahead first.

The Fox Inn (01869 345284) in Souldern is both a pub and a bed and breakfast and is well known for its dining, including both lunches and evening meals, and prides itself for maintaining the best traditions of an English countryside inn. Nearby Fritwell has the Kings Head (01869 346738). Originally built as three cottages this was converted into an inn in 1735. The pub has polished wooden floors and low beamed ceilings as well as an open fire in the winter. The landlord takes care to serve the local Hook Norton bitter and, unusually for a pub, food focuses on the collaboration with the 'Wing Fung' restaurant to offer a selection of Chinese dishes. Traditionally, Fritwell has had a second pub, the George and Dragon, but at the time of writing this was boarded up and untenanted.

The Red Lion (01869 340225) in Steeple Aston was rescued from pub-chain homogenisation by its present owners, who strive to preserve the ideal of a traditional village pub focusing on beer and banter rather than fancy meals and gaming machines. That said, the pub does offer food, which it describes as 'Honest English Cuisine' although not on Sundays, and all food is prepared to order, so it's not a place to come if you're in a hurry. The other 'horse' in Steeple Aston is the White Horse (01869 340307), which serves Morrells ales and is a good old village pub.

The Barley Mow in Upper Heyford (01869 232300) is small and convivial but does not offer food and those looking to eat should aim for The Bell in Lower Heyford (01869 347176), which has a good menu and is welcoming to boaters and out-of-towners.

There is a choice of three pubs in Tackey; The Kings Arms (01869 331334), which is a basic local; Sturdy's Castle (01869 331328) and The Gardiner Arms (01869 331266). The latter is the most significant of these being family run and offering a good menu of home-cooked dishes. This pub not only has an Aunt Sally but also a skittles alley, another Oxfordshire speciality, as well as a kids' area and beer garden. Sturdy's Castle is a little out of the village to the west on the A4260.

The Oxford Arms in Kirtlington (01869 350208) next door to the village store has become one of the main focal points for the village since. Recently taken over by a small chain, the pub has a restaurant and also offers bar snacks. At the time of writing the second pub

The Black's Head is a common pub name in these parts and refers to a type of sheep.

in the village, the Dashwood Arms, was covered with scaffolding and it was unclear whether it was being renovated or converted.

Finally, the Black's Head in Bletchingdon (01869 350315) is at the heart of the village on the main road going through it and opposite the shaded green. The pub has a pleasant patio at the rear and offers a range of food.

SLEEPING

This section offers a good range of village based bed and breakfasts as well as a couple of hotels and some campsites.

HOTELS

The two hotels are:

- **The Holt Hotel** near Steeple Aston (01869 340259) – *a refurbished coaching inn with eighty-six rooms, dating back to the fifteenth century. The hotel offers a range of accommodation from single to four-poster bedrooms.*

- **The Oxfordshire Inn**, Heathfield Village near Bletchingdon, just off the A34 (01869 351444) – *a converted sixteenth-century barn with a selection of functional double, twin or family rooms.*

BED AND BREAKFAST/GUESTHOUSES

Those looking for somewhere for overnight or short stays with the chance to meet some locals are advised to go for one of the many bed and breakfasts and pubs offering rooms in the district, of which the following represents a selection:

- **The Fox Inn** at Souldern (01869 345284) – *a local pub offering a choice of four rooms.*

- **Tower Fields**, Souldern (01869 346554) – *offering a choice of three rooms.*

Tackley Manor gate and church.

SECTION D

Ayhno Viaduct, from the canal.

- **Home Farm House,** Middle Aston (01869 340666) – *rooms in a seventeenth-century former farmhouse.*
- **Westfield Farm Motel,** Steeple Aston (01869 340591) – *a converted stable block with en-suite bedroom units and a combined lounge/dining room and bar.*
- **Colliers,** Tackley (01869 331255)
– *can also offer stabling for horses.*
- **Vicarage Farmhouse,** Kirtlington (01869 350254) – *rooms in a modern farmhouse.*
- **The Black's Head** in Bletchingdon (01869 350315) – *bed and breakfast accommodation as well as the food and drink you'd expect of a village pub.*

Just off the map there are B&Bs at **The Old Post Office** in Ardeley (01869 345958) and **Westfield Court House** in Weston on the Green east of Bletchingdon (01869 350777).

CAMPING
There is a choice of three campsites in this section:

- **Diamond Farm Caravan & Camping Park,** Heathfield, Bletchingdon (01869 350909) – *a small family-run site with good facilities.*
- **Heyford Leys Farm,** near Upper Heyford (01869 232048) – *another*
family-run park on an old seventeenth-century farm.
- **Lince Copse Caravan and Camping Park,** Enslow Wharf near Gibraltar and Kirtlington and on the canal (01869 331508).

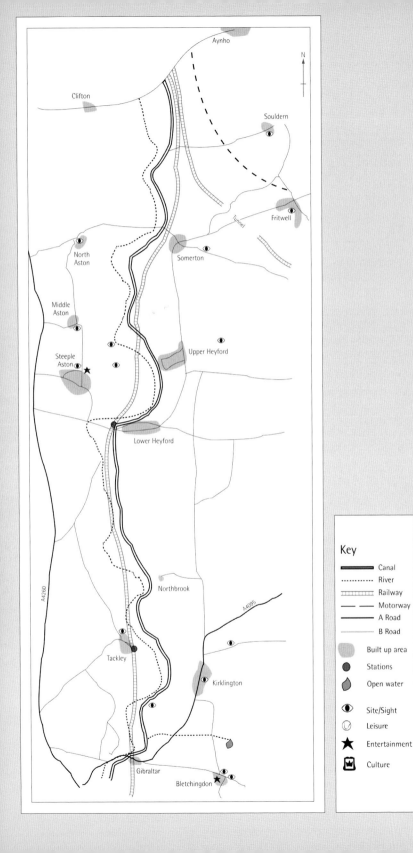

Aynho

Clifton

Souldern

Fritwell

Tunnel

North
Aston

Somerton

Middle
Aston

Steeple
Aston

Upper Heyford

Lower Heyford

Northbrook

A4260

A4095

Tackley

Kirklington

Gibraltar

Bletchingdon

Key

—— Canal

········· River

▦▦▦▦ Railway

– – – Motorway

—— A Road

—— B Road

Built up area

Stations

Open water

Site/Sight

Leisure

Entertainment

Culture

SEEING AND DOING

INTRODUCTION

There is no shortage of historical and more modern curiosities to seek out along this stretch, with many a surprising find waiting to be unearthed. By spending a little time to linger, it is possible to tune in to the accidents of birth, geography and history that have helped to mould the character of the villages along the way. The same applies when it comes to seeking cultural stimulation or entertainment. Much is 'home-grown' and should be viewed on that level. When the time comes for something more sophisticated or grand, it is then that Banbury and Oxford don't seem so far away.

SIGHTS

The church of St Mary the Virgin in Souldern was where William Wordsworth stayed with his friend Robert Jones, the rector there, and where he wrote his poem *A Parsonage in Oxfordshire.*

St Olaves church, Fritwell, was named after St Olaf the Christian King of Norway and a Viking warrior, by the Normans who founded the church. It served the village well until the middle nineteenth century by which time the fabric had fallen into such a poor condition that it was described as 'unfit for public worship'. Salvation came in the shape of a rich new vicar, Samuel Yorke, who paid for £2,000 worth of restoration. Whilst this saved the building, it was at the cost of losing much of the original architecture.

In the chancel of St Olaf's there is a mis-spelt brass plaque that records a bequest of 40s a year to the poor of Fritwell, a tradition that continues to this day.

St Olave's lychgate, which was possibly erected to compensate for the otherwise very unprepossessing main door, was presented as a gift by the 1st Viscount Simon who was Lord High Chancellor and lived in the manor house opposite the church from 1911-1932. It was dedicated by the Archbishop of York in 1922.

Mazes, including those made out of turf, became very fashionable during Queen Elizabeth's reign when they became known as 'Troy Towns', in deference to the Trojan myths, or 'Julian's Bowers'.

The otherwise modest village of Somerton has a couple of gems hidden away, not least its turf maze, which is no tiddler at over 60ft. It sits on private land 1.5 miles east south-east of Somerton at Troy Farm and is surrounded by a tall hedge and can be viewed if permission is gained beforehand.

Somerton also has the site of a medieval castle, chapel and fishponds, with the remains of the chapel at least visible in the modern

A wartime pill box at Somerton.

One of a series of wooden sculptures at Somerton.

schoolhouse. Otherwise it is only the site that can be seen down the lane past the church.

North Aston is worth pausing in, if only briefly, to note how it clusters round a green, and how the village is quite clearly distinct from the traditional focal points of the church and manorial hall, which sit in splendid isolation in parkland to the east. The reason for this is that the village was abandoned from its original position in the fifteenth century. A similar fate was endured by the village of Nethercote around the same time, when the enclosures led to land being given over to sheep. All that remains of a community that existed for over 500 years is the present-day Grange Farm.

Whilst in North Aston look out for the sign on the green which was designed and carved in the village and portrays four notable characters from the village's past. Also look out for the wonderful public tap in the wall nearby.

Middle Aston Manor House can be seen from the corner of the road connecting Steeple and North Aston is now a training centre. Look hard and you may spot a few participants being put through their paces in team building exercises in the grounds.

The Steeple Aston Cope in the church of St Peter and St Paul is a semi-circular ecclesiastical cloak embroidered in the early fourteenth century. This is renowned as one of the finest examples of embroidery from the Middle Ages at a time when English embroiderers were the finest in Europe. Now a dull tan colour, in its time the Cope would have been a collection of bright pinks and reds with gold and silver thread. The original is in the Victoria and Albert Museum, but a corner of the church

North Aston's public taps.

is dedicated to illustrations of the Cope as well as further explanation as to its significance. Also in the church is a second chapel with a tomb dedicated to Frances, Lady Page, as well as her husband Sir Francis Page, the notorious 'hanging judge' of the eighteenth century. Finally, the church has a good example of a wooden screen.

> In his time Page's power was such that he was able to impose his will upon the local clergy. He restored the Lady Chapel, separated it from the rest of the church and placed a marble tomb, which is completely out of character, inside. It remains there today.

Between Steeple Aston and Upper Heyford look out for the Eyecatcher in the fields. A three-arched folly, this was designed by William Kent to be part of Rousham Park and is best seen by going down Cow Lane from Steeple Aston and following the footpath around Folly Field.

Rousham Park (01869 347110) itself is best known for its grounds, which represent the last undisturbed garden laid out by William Kent (1685-1748), and offer an excellent example of the first phase of English landscape gardening. It can be enjoyed as Kent intended, as a garden that uses and magnifies its natural setting. Key features include Venus's Vale with cascades and ponds and the Praeneste, a seven-arched portico from which one can sit and look over the park towards the Eyecatcher. There's also a walled garden with herbaceous borders with a rare form of shaggy longhorn cattle wandering about on the other side of the ha-ha.

Rousham House itself is also worth a visit, although it is open less frequently than the park. Built in 1635 by Sir Robert Dormer, it is still owned by the same family and although retaining much of its original charm it was altered during the Victorian period, and not always for the better.

Tackley is notable for the archway left standing on the green by John Harborne, a London merchant who bought the local manor in 1612. Although his house is long gone the archway, complete with his coat of arms, remains as his memorial, along with three fishponds, which are now listed as an ancient monument. Two of these are triangular in shape with the third square and they are considered classics of their type. They sit on private land between the station and the green in the grounds of Court Farm House, but can occasionally be seen when the gardens open as part of the National Gardens Scheme.

Another member of the Morton family was said to be the inspiration for the famous W.F. Yeames picture 'When Did You Last See Your Father?' showing a young boy being interrogated by Roundheads during the Civil War, with the father in question being Sir William Morton, who escaped from the Tower in 1645.

Water seems to be a theme in Tackley, which also has a series of lakes in the park to the south near Hill Court. These were created in 1773 by John Morton, who was following the fashion started at nearby Blenheim for damming a spring in order to create a landscape feature. The Mortons remained in Tackley for four generations.

The name of Upper Heyford became synonymous with its airfield during the 1980s when it became a key strategic NATO base with a strong USAF presence. The base was originally opened during the First World War and leased to the Americans when it was no longer needed until 1993 when it passed back to the RAF. Today the site is a large industrial estate known as Heyford Park, although much of the airfield remains in mothballs and evidence of its previous use is still very much on view, although visitors are not encouraged to linger!

The site is a mix of 1930s buildings and fifty-six so-called Hardened Aircraft Shelters, built by NATO as part of its policy of strengthening key bases. Another key building is the old Command Centre, an ugly concrete affair that has been scheduled by English Heritage and may one day become a museum. Completely windowless, this monstrosity offers a bleak reminder of a time when the Cold War was at freezing point.

Between Gibraltar and Kirtlington lies Kirtlington Quarry, these days a Site of Special Scientific Interest but until recently the property of Blue Circle Cement. During its quarrying years the company exposed a wealth of geology that can now be appreciated by the public. Limestone, marls and clays deposited during the Middle Jurassic period about 172 million years ago – a time when this part of the world was part of a warm shallow sea, possibly populated by a number of small islands – are on view. Evidence for the latter includes the discovery of some dinosaur skeletons and fossilised wood. Others fossils discovered here include those of rare mammals from the Mesozoic period. Fossil collecting over the years, combined with other activities such as motorcycle scrambling, paid their toll and Blue Circle Cement now lease the site to Cherwell District Council who maintain it as a nature reserve, accessible by road or canal.

The church of St Mary the Virgin Kirtlington is well worth a visit. Records show that there was a church here before King Edward held a Royal Council in Kirtlington in 977, although the fabric of the 'modern' church dates back mainly to the middle ages. That said, it is a hotchpotch of building styles, ranging from Saxon through to a late Victorian Gothic chancel.

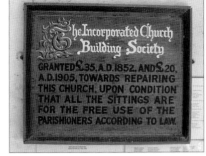

This sign in Kirtlington church shows how rebuilding is a constant problem.

The church's most striking feature is probably the Dashwood side chapel, opposite which there's a glass bookcase showing old documents such as a 1911 edition of the *Churchman's Almanack*, a *Book of Common Services* dated 1839 and old parish magazines. The church also boasts its own ancient wall painting and some splendid stained glass. The list of vicars behind the choir stalls goes back to 1096.

Few of the predominately early eighteenth-century gravestones in the immediate vicinity of St Mary's churchyard have survived, whilst those that have are severely weathered, and on first impressions this area can appear unkempt. It is worth a second look though as a substantial part of the churchyard is being managed as part of the 'Living Churchyard Project' with the aim of preserving wildlife, both flora and fauna, including wild flowers, butterflies, birds, plants and insects. There is a list of the various species of both that abound in the space, such as Red Campion and Mouse-Ear Hawkweed. The churchyard is best seen in spring, but is worth a visit at any time of year.

The eighteenth-century grand Palladian mansion of Kirtlington Park near the polo ground can just be glimpsed between the trees and was, perhaps inevitably, laid out by Capability Brown. The house boasts a classical portico and two oak staircases, but if you want to view them your best chance is to go to a weeding here, as this is when it is open to the public.

The church at Bletchingdon, St Giles, is also worth seeing. Although the church itself is usually kept locked you can put your head round the porch to see an old wooden funeral cart in the porch. The graveyard has spilled over into a separate walled area guarded by a large arch, but you might spot an unusual Celtic cross outside dedicated to the memory of a captain in the Royal Hussars who died in Ypres in 1914.

St Giles lies slightly out of the village and is linked to the main collection of houses by a public footpath, from which you can see the back of the glorious Bletchingdon Park and the majestic lawns sweeping up to it. Back in the heart of the village, note the old blacksmith's shop,

SECTION D

the only building on the green, and if you're looking to satisfy a thirst as well as historical curiosity its worth popping into the Black's Head

Funeral cart, Bletchingdon.

where there's an old oak beamed window frame that was recovered from earlier building work hanging from one of the walls and has been dated back to 1550-1650.

Slightly off the map to the west is Woodstock, which is worth visiting for a number of reasons, the most obvious of which is probably the set-piece grandeur of Blenheim Palace. Designed by Sir John Vanbrugh for John Churchill, 1st Duke of Marlborough, Blenheim was largely paid for by the nation in gratitude for the Duke's victory over the French and Bavarians at

Blenheim in 1704, although a later falling-out between the then Queen and Marlborough's widow meant that building was put on hold for some time.

> Blenheim is, of course, where Sir Winston Churchill was born, and his grave can be seen in the churchyard of the nearby village of Blaydon.

The current Blenheim is therefore relatively modern, although it was built on the site of Woodstock Manor House, a royal residence for centuries. Records show the old house was a burden on the exchequer of both Henry II and III with the latter alone spending £3,300 on it. By 1272 there were extensive royal apartments and kitchens, six chapels and a canopied throne in the hallway.

Woodstock's antecedents go back even further than that

> In the village of Stonesfield near Woodstock stone used to be quarried underground between Michaelmas and Christmas Day and then covered over with turves. As soon as a hard frost was likely the church bells would ring and all the men from the village would turn out to expose the stone and let the frost split it ready for shaping. The result was highly valued and can be seen on many local properties.

however. Before the Norman Conquest, when the Wychwood Forest stretched from the Cotswolds to London, English kings had lodges in Woodstock, which translates as 'a clearing in the woods'. King Alfred is reputed to have stayed at Woodstock in 890 and Ethelred the Unready held a council in the town suggesting its size had grown fit to accommodate a king. Today, the deer park surrounding the house can be accessed by public footpath as can some of the gardens, which were landscaped by Capability Brown in 1760.

Today Woodstock remains a local community, although these days tourism and quaintness remain its main assets rather than the glove making from which it once earned its living. The Town Hall is eighteenth century and there are numerous attractive period buildings,

Upper Heyford.

including the seventeenth-century Fletcher's house, now home to the County Museum. Chaucer's House in Park Street was once home to Chaucer the poet.

CULTURE AND ENTERTAINMENT

A number of the pubs in this section run regular folk clubs, with good examples being the Black's Head in Bletchingdon, the Rock of Gibraltar and the White Lion in Steeple Aston (see Basics). There is a tendency for the villages to be fairly self-contained entertainment-wise, and it can be worth consulting local notice boards or posters stuck up on telegraph poles to see what's coming up. You may be surprised by the variety.

Most of the villages in this section also have their own playing fields and children's play equipment, with particularly impressive sets available on the outskirts of Souldern and by the village hall in Tackley, whilst those in Lower Heyford, just the other side of the lift bridge, are conveniently located for boaters with children needing to run off a bit of energy.

SECTION D

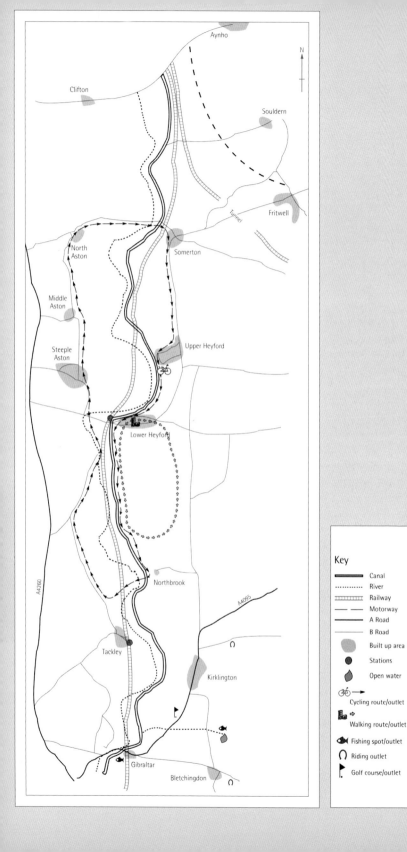

Aynho

Clifton

Souldern

Fritwell

Tunnel

North
Aston

Somerton

Middle
Aston

Upper Heyford

Steeple
Aston

Lower Heyford

Northbrook

A4260

A4095

Tackley

Kirklington

Gibraltar

Bletchingdon

N

Key

━━━ Canal
‥‥‥ River
▦▦▦ Railway
━ ━ Motorway
━━ A Road
━━ B Road
🟫 Built up area
🔵 Stations
💧 Open water
🚲➙ Cycling route/outlet
🏭⇨ Walking route/outlet
🐟 Fishing spot/outlet
∩ Riding outlet
🚩 Golf course/outlet

SAMPLING

INTRODUCTION

This section is well blessed with public rights of way to allow you to enjoy the countryside, including a number of long-distance trails as well as a Sustrans national cycle network. In addition, there's no shortage of bridleways, although opportunities for fishing are confined to the canal and River Cherwell.

The OS Explorer Maps covering this section are number 191 Banbury, Bicester and Chipping Norton (East sheet) and number 180 Oxford (East and West sheets).

WALKING

There is a good selection of footpaths along this stretch, although those that run up from the canal inevitably involve some gradients and may not be suitable for some people. This is more true of those that lie to the west of the water, running along or near to the ridge which hosts the Astons.

> Aves Ditch, running north-east from Kirtlington towards the old Upper Heyford airbase, is thought to be an old Iron Age boundary. Most of this is tree-lined and the whole length is a public highway.

East of the canal the old Upper Heyford airbase acts as a not-so-natural barrier for walkers, and a glance at the map reveals a number of thoroughfares that have a gap in the middle where the base now stands. However, shorter circular walks through or near the various villages are possible.

Cherwell District Council has produced a leaflet called Cherwell Valley Walks which can either be bought or downloaded off their website www.cherwelldc.gov.uk. This leaflet describes a marked 14-mile route that passes through Lower Heyford, the Astons and the outskirts of Somerton before returning along the towpath, pointing out places of interest along the way (see Learn More and Links). The same leaflet also gives a short 2-mile circular walk through the Heyfords.

The Roman Akeman Street lining Corinium (modern-day Cirencester) and Verulamium (St Albans) also passes through this section to the south of Tackley, where it is part of the Oxfordshire Way, before becoming the road heading northeast out of Kirtlington past the polo ground. The A4260 to the west of the section has also been a long-distance thoroughfare since prehistoric times.

Walk D begins at The Bell in Lower Heyford and passes down the canal towpath for a couple of miles before climbing up the hills to the east of the canal to give a good view over the Cherwell Valley and over fields back to Lower Heyford.

SECTION D WALK

From Lower Heyford and Back via Dashwoods Lock

Description:	*A good way to appreciate the canal both at water level and from some of the hills that line its eastern bank.*
Distance:	*4.5 miles*
Duration:	*2hrs*
Staring point:	*Grid Reference 486247, OS Explorer 191 (E)*
Nearest Refreshment:	*The Bell, Lower Heyford*

Turn left out of the pub and head down Freehold Street, past the phone box and then left when the road forks down Mill Lane towards the canal. Cross over the lift bridge and pick up the towpath to your left. Pass the railway station and go through a pleasantly wooded section of the canal, which eventually opens out just at the point where the railway scoots away to the right.

Shortly after this you will pass under a bridge, where the towpath becomes less solid and altogether more bumpy. You soon reach Dashwoods Lock, however, where you should leave the canal and cross over and take the second (right hand) of two metal gates. Pass up the left-hand side of this field where you meet another gate. Pass through this and into another field, where you turn left and keep the hedge to your left. You should now be walking parallel to the canal but in the opposite direction.

Continue in the same direction past the abandoned farm and keep with the path as it goes around a bend and then past a metal barn. About 200yds after this the path forks and you need to take the narrower path cutting diagonally across the corner of the field to your left. At the bottom of the field cross over the road, pass over a stile and across a meadow. The path then passes through a latched kissing gate and finally through another wooden gate where you emerge once more on Freehold Street. Turn left and you soon come back to the pub.

SECTION D

The best place to look for walking equipment and supplies is either Bicester or Oxford (see Section E).

CYCLING

The National Cycle Route 5, running from Oxford to Birmingham, passes close to this section, coming through Woodstock to the west and then up to Banbury. The Oxfordshire Cycleway, also Route 5, is signed and passes through Bletchingdon, Kirtlington, Upper Heyford and Somerton (see Learn More and Links).

Cycling alongside the canal is probably best done along the stretch south of Upper Heyford, although the towpath can become bumpy and uncomfortable at any point in this section. Given the beauty of the local countryside, the best way of sampling this section on two wheels is possibly by staying on-road but using some of the more minor roads that link the villages along the way.

One suggested route begins at Upper Heyford and picks up the canal at Allen's Bridge (Number 204) just to the south of Allen's Lock before heading south, past the back of Lower Heyford and past Dashwood Lock before reaching Northbrook Bridge (Number 210), just before Northbrook Lock. Turn right here, heading west then south along a bridleway until you reach the outskirts of Tackley where you need to turn right and head downhill and north towards a T-junction, where you turn right and head towards Rousham Park.

Continue straight on at the crossroads at Heyford Bridge and head into Steeple Aston by turning right at the stores. Go down the dip and up again into Middle and then North Aston, taking care to take the turn right at the first of these just after the grounds of Middle Aston House.

On reaching North Aston turn right again and head downhill towards the river, then cross the canal at Bridge 196, before climbing again into Somerton, although the canal is a good place to stop to catch your breath. Continue on the main road through Somerton and you will return to your starting point at Upper Heyford. This route will then have taken you through many of the villages on this section over a total course of approximately 14 miles.

The nearest bike supplies are to be found in Oxford where there is a wealth of choice (see Section E).

RIDING

There are a number of good bridleways in this section, notably one linking Kirtlington and Lower Heyford and one starting near Upper Heyford and passing to the west of Fritwell before linking up with Souldern. Part of the 50-mile Claude Du Val Bridleway also passes through this section at Tackley (see the British Horse Society in 'Learn More and Links').

There are not one but two polo grounds in this section, one outside Bletchingdon at **Heathfeld Park**, just off the A34 (01869 351111) and the more famous **Kirtlington Polo Club** (01869 350138) on the edge of that village, which is of international standard. Near to this section the annual Blenheim Horse Trials are held every September at Blenheim Palace just outside Woodstock.

Riding establishments and suppliers along this stretch include: **Asker Horse Sports**, Heathfield Village, near Bletchingdon (01869 351111) – *show equipment, show jumps.*

FISHING

Fishing along this stretch is confined mainly to the canal and the River Cherwell, but there are plenty of spots to choose from.

Recommended pitches on the canal are:

- **Allen's Lock**, Upper Heyford – *mainly smaller fish such as dace and chubb, although larger carp are not unknown. (Controlled by Banbury and District AA).*
- **Bletchingdon** (The Rock of Gibraltar) – *some good quality chub up near the turning point north of the pub, with bream up to 4lbs and roach up to 2lbs. Tench and carp can also be found where the bankside becomes more reed-lined further up. (Controlled by Oxford and District AA).*

Recommended spots on the river include:

- **Bletchingdon** (The Rock of Gibraltar) – *chub, tench and bream around 6-7lbs with the occasional large carp. (Controlled by Banbury and District AA).*
- **Upper Heyford** – *roach and chub with some pike with some good pools. (Controlled by Banbury and District AA).*
- **Northbrook** – *from 250yds below Dashwood Lock to 100yds below Northbrook Lock. (Controlled by Oxford and District AA).*
- **Three Pigeons Lock**, Kirtlington – *from 300yds below Bridge 212 to Flights Mill above the lock (Controlled by Oxford and District AA).*
- **Northbrook** – *canal side from 50yds downstream of the first canal bridge downstream of the lock, to meadow past railway bridge approximately 1 mile upstream of lock. (Controlled by Bicester and District AA).*

There is also good fishing to be had at **Manor Lake** near Kirtlington (01869 345486), a traditional estate lake fishery of around 8 acres surrounded by mature willow and chestnut trees. Carp up to 20lb are available from the wooden landing stages as well as tench, bream, roach, rudd and pike. Day tickets must be purchased in advance from J&K Tackle.

Fishing supplies are probably best obtained in either Oxford or Bicester. Outlets include **J&K Tackle**, 62-64 Sheep Street, Bicester (01869 244143).

OTHER

There is one golf course on this stretch; **Kirtlington Golf Club**, on the southern approach to Kirtlington (D2 01819 351133) – 18 holes, 6,084yds. The course also has a driving range. In addition, there is a golf centre with a driving range at Heathfield village just off the A34 near Bletchingdon (01869 351552).

GIBRALTAR
TO OXFORD

Key

═══	Canal		Built up area	○	Turning point
·········	River	●	Stations	⋀	Lock
▥▥▥	Railway	◆	Open water	Ⓑ	Boatyard
— —	Motorway			W	Waterpoint
───	A Road				
───	B Road				

SHAPERS

THE CANAL ON THIS STRETCH

KEY FACTS

LENGTH: 8.5 miles

BOATYARDS: 2
- College Cruisers
- Castlemill Boatyard

WATERPOINTS: 6
- Thrupp Bridge
- Langford Lane Bridge
- Duke's Bridge
- Perry's Lift Bridge
- St Edwards Lift Bridge
- Terminus

TURNING POINTS: 5
- Cherwell below Baker's Bridge
- Cherwell above Shipton Weir Lock
- Thrupp
- Duke's Lock
- Terminus

LOCKS: 6
- Bakers Lock (8ft 6in)
- Shipton Weir (2ft 5in)
- Roundham Lock (7ft 5in)
- Kidlington Green (4ft 9in)
- Duke's Lock (5ft 4in)
- Wolvercote (3ft 8in)

After the excitement of 'The Wides' and the tranquillity of Thrupp, the canal begins its steady descent into Oxford via Kidlington, with the landscape increasingly dominated by industrial scenes and busy roads that contrast with the largely rural nature of the canal to this point. The long run in to Oxford itself is marked by a conservation area, which means that mooring is restricted to long-term permit holders and tends to lead to some 'bunching up' near the terminus itself.

After Blake's Lock the canal and river become one, with an indicator board just above the lock giving an idea of the state of the current, which can be severe and needs to be respected. This section of the waterway is know locally as 'The Wides', but could just as easily be called The Bends.

> The cement works behind 'The Wides' includes a tall chimney known locally as 'Smokey Joe'.

> Not surprisingly, given its proximity to the canal, Shipton's church was once known as the bargees' church.

Here the course is unmistakably the river's, with a series of meanders both lending character and requiring those on tiller duty to exercise previously under-used muscles to navigate a successful course. Mooring is difficult due to high bankside growth, but the compensation of this is a rich variety of wildlife.

The lozenge-shaped Shipton Weir Lock brings you back onto the canal proper after which there is a wide sweep to the right and the last of three railway bridges. Shipton on Cherwell's church looks down on the canal from the right, guarding the territory of the highly organised Thrupp Canal Cruising Club, the first of whose members line a long stretch of long-term mooring on the left. The popularity of Thrupp is well earned, and the sheer number of boats, many of which are highly coloured and well maintained, is a feast for the eyes.

The actual approach into Thrupp is almost river-like in appearance and ends in a sharp bend to the right where there is also a lift bridge. It is possible to turn here if you're careful and the unmanned Thrupp yard offers a water point. Short-term moorings after the bridge are policed enthusiastically by volunteers from the Cruising Club, but even so spaces can be hard to come by in the summer.

The pattern of moored boats continues beyond Thrupp almost as far as a second sharp bend to the right, also accompanied by a water point, at the northern point of Kidlington. The respite is brief however as another spate of long-term moorings follows after the bend, with the boats here having a slightly more 'lived in' look than those in the heart of Thrupp.

The towpath is firm here, although the views to the right are mainly hidden by trees, which is no great loss as they mirror those on the other side, namely the back of industrial units, which fade after the red-bricked Bridge 225. Roundham Lock breaks a long straight in two and the towpath definitely takes on a more rural feel around this point.

Open fields and meadows appear on the right, along with a number of pretty stone bridges carrying country lanes into the town to the left. The towpath retains its solid nature and is mostly easy going from here into Oxford. Kidlington Green Lock has a seat for walkers and is significant for marking the end of Kidlington.

Another long straight follows, broken by a kink at King's Bridge. Mooring is possible along this stretch but occasionally treacherous. There is some formal mooring in the run up to Drinkwater's Lift Bridge, where a sign somewhat prematurely welcomes you to Oxford. After this

Duke's Cut, one of the entry points to the Thames.

there are some 14-day moorings complete with water point followed by some more long-term moorings.

Duke's Lock and Bridge appear, with a turn to the right offering the first of two entry points onto the Thames and has the added attraction of passing through the delightful Oxey Mead Wildlife Sanctuary with its variety of bird life, including kingfishers. The towpath bridge also sports one of the RBS Millennium Cycleway signposts.

> Duke's Cut is named after the Duke of Marlborough who owned the paper mills at Wolvercote and did a deal with the canal's engineers to construct a cut between the River Thames and the canal to ease access.

The canal now passes under two concrete bridges holding the A40 and the A34 respectively and then under two lift bridges which are usually down (Numbers 233 and 234). There's a water point just after the second of these and some Agenda 21 moorings afterwards. A long straight follows Wolvercote Lock, after which there are sporadic 48-hour moorings.

> Agenda 21 takes its name from a UN initiative designed to encourage sustainable development.

The run in to Oxford is marked by a long stretch of Conservation Area where mooring is not permitted except on the exceptional visitor moorings. Although laudable, the practical effect of this for the boater is that they are left with little choice but to plough on to Oxford. There are water points and even refuse points, but these are primarily for the use of those living along this section.

For the walker or cyclist the towpath is made up and therefore easy going. Just before entering the city itself there's an interesting

SECTION E

Oxford College cruisers and St Barnabas church.

diversion at the Trap Grounds, an area of scrubland that survives to give an idea of what all the land around Oxford used to look like. It is significant for being a wetland habitat where thirty-five different types of bird nest, including the rare Water Rail.

The canal now runs along the backs of houses on the opposite bank and has a large expanse of open ground to stretch your legs just after Bridge 241. The houses give way to a run of industrial buildings the style of which has been replicated in some modern flats.

A long line of 48-hour moorings follows and this stretch is often very busy with craft. College cruisers follows on the opposite bank with the magnificent St Barnabas church towering over it, and a stream comes up alongside the canal on the towpath side, followed shortly after by the Castlemill Boatyard.

The end of the canal is indeed now nigh. There is a 50ft turning point just in front of Isis Lock which provides the second access point to the Thames. The combination of the river, hirers from college cruisers doing their first lock and the turning point can be an interesting one at times. The canal isn't quite done – it continues for another hundred yards or so the other side of a turnover bridge, although given that the maximum wind at the very end is 30ft, most of these must reverse into their berth. In reality few probably move that much if the evidence of cultivated gardens on the towpath is anything to go by. Then, like many canals, the water stops abruptly and the city begins.

PRINCIPAL TOWNS AND VILLAGES ON THIS STRETCH

BEGBROKE

Grouped to the east of the A44, on the other side of which sits Begbroke Priory, the village's focal point for centuries and still an active institution today which occasionally holds open days. For a long time there were no less than three manor houses here, but little in the way of peasantry. Begbroke has grown rapidly since the 1930s due largely to the development of a commercial estate specialising in hi-tech research and development.

> Begbroke's name is derived from two Anglo-Saxon words meaning stream and archaeologists have found evidence of settlement dating back to pre-Christian times.

CUTTESLOWE

A district of Oxford based around a 1930s housing estate of mainly red-bricked semis and terraces surrounded by more suburban dwellings. Tucked away in the northeast corner of the city, Cutteslowe is also known for its large park which as well as playing host to a range of events also acts as the city's main public park with playing fields, a large pond and even a miniature railway.

> Cutteslowe is infamous for its Cutteslowe Walls, a sort of Berlin Wall erected by a property developer to 'protect' private housing from a feared influx of slum clearance council tenants. The Walls were the subject of numerous legal battles and stood for twenty years.

HAMPTON GAY

An isolated settlement consisting of no more than a farm and a few attached cottages down the end of a long, single-track road.

HAMPTON POYLE

A small village of relatively modern housing clustered in a bend in the road, although the church is at the end of its own track.

KIDLINGTON

Reputedly the largest village in England, despite repeated attempts by its residents to have it classified as a town. Although Kidlington's heart still beats with historical reminders of its village roots (it was originally known as Kidlington on the Green), recent development including shopping centres and a large supermarket on the outskirts, as well as the creation of Kidlington Garden City to the south, make it a vibrant community. The headquarters of both the County Fire Service and Thames Valley Police are here.

OXFORD

Part centre of learning, part a living tourist destination, part regional centre and part industrial centre, Oxford lives a diverse existence. It is the university that dominates, with thirty-nine colleges, each operating as a self-contained community, although it can be hard for the outsider to decipher the intricate code of what is what and who is where. The Cotswolds' characteristic honey-coloured stone is used throughout giving the city a uniform appearance. The centre is compact but has all the facilities you'd expect of a major city, whilst the outskirts are clustered into a series of distinct communities, each with their own identity.

> The lake at Shipton Manor was created by its owner Richard Branson, when he dammed a small stream that formed the village boundary.

SHIPTON ON CHERWELL

A pretty village of two halves. The first is dominated by high stone walls behind which sit two large houses, one with its own lake. The second is a modern housing estate.

One of the two Manor Houses in Shipton on Cherwell.

SUMMERTOWN

A middle-class outpost of Oxford much beloved of academics and those seeking easy access to the numerous private schools scattered nearby. Summertown's heart is a parade of shops on the Banbury Road, which is mainly post-war in nature and has little to recommend it. Surrounding streets have a mix of Victorian and Edwardian semis and terraced housing, with more modern apartment blocks and student accommodation thrown in.

There has been a mill at Thrupp since the Norman Conquest, and it was eventually bought by the canal company in 1790 to help supply the final stretch of the waterway down to Oxford with water. Today it is owned by British Waterways and can be found near the water point.

THRUPP

Not really much more than a very picturesque run of cottages along the side of the canal. The presence of a pub and the activism of the Cruising Club give the community something to coalesce around.

As far ago as 1718 it was remarked that 'some of the best paper made in England is made at Wolvercote Mill.' The village had a reliable source of waterpower and, from the beginning of the nineteenth century, a constant source of coal for power from the canal.

WOLVERCOTE

A split community divided into Upper and Lower halves and separated by the canal. The former has the primary school, shop and social housing, as well as the church, although this was rebuilt in 1860. Lower Wolvercote is altogether more genteel and runs from the Green to the Trout Inn, much featured in *Inspector Morse*, as well as a number of other old pubs and a 300-year-old paper mill.

YARNTON

Yarnton is grouped to the west of the A44, on a point north of its original location by the church and manor house. The village has seen much recent development including a small industrial estate and thrives as an out of town location a short drive from Oxford.

> In its original location, Yarnton had hay meadows sweeping down to the Thames. Until as late as 1978 mowing rights were allocated by lots using rosewood balls, which still survive.

HISTORY

Although the fortunes of the city of Oxford have tended to dominate local history for the last thousand years this has not always been the case. The village of Yarnton has some claims to be one of the earliest inhabited settlements in the country, with recent excavations suggesting there has been a community here since 3500 BC.

Certainly by Saxon times many of the villages we know today were at least established, although it would probably be a mistake to describe them as thriving. The history of these villages before and after the Norman Conquest was basically one of struggle and survival.

As if coping with the vicissitudes nature wasn't enough, villages also had to deal with the whims of local landowners. Just after the Norman Conquest the Hampton estates of Gay and Poyle, for example, were both owned by the de Gay family who acted as lords of the manor. During the ten years either side of 1200, Osney Abbey near Oxford began to acquire land in the vicinity and Robert de Gay began to turn some of his land over to the church.

As a result of this the manor itself soon transferred to the Abbey who held it until the Dissolution. Kidlington was also held by Osney Abbey and following the Dissolution both this village and many of those surrounding it faced an uncertain period.

There were widespread revolts in Elizabethan times when land enclosures threatened (and often succeeded) in unsettling the precarious balancing act that was agrarian survival. In 1596 a call to arms amongst those tilling the soil in Hampton Gay resulted in ten men turning up on Enslow Hill in Bletchingdon to fight for their rights. Five were arrested and one sent to London to be hanged and quartered.

Evidence of prehistoric settlement in Oxford includes Iron Age ditches and Bronze Age barrows around Port Meadow as well as close to the Parks and in modern-day Cowley. Neolithic settlements are also thought to have existed where Christ Church stands today, and in Wolvercote.

Sited on the borders of Mercia and Wessex, and with the Thames providing access to the sea, Oxford was an obvious focus for development.

SECTION E

The town's growing importance was confirmed in the eighth century with the founding of a nunnery.

After a period under Mercian rule the town grew rapidly under Edward the Elder, son of Alfred the Great, and although it suffered the ignominy of being burned down by invading Danes in 979 Oxford's location meant that it had become a national centre and by the eleventh century assemblies were held in the town. It was here in 1020 that the Danes and the English were brought together under Canute and, sixteen years later, where his son Harold was proclaimed king.

Around this time Oxford stood on a par with London and before the Conquest was actually the capital. The Domesday Book acknowledges the town as one of the largest in the kingdom but equally recorded that much of the land was laid to waste, suggesting it might not have passed quietly to the invader.

This theory is substantiated by the fact that Robert d'Oilly who was granted the town began his ownership by acting as a stern ruler, although in time he softened and became a great benefactor. The town became a royal favourite of Henry I and Oxford Castle reinforced the town's strategic importance, as did the building of a hunting lodge at nearby Woodstock. This event was to have a significant impact upon the local area, the road between Oxford and Woodstock frequently witnessing the passage of a royal train.

Students began to arrive in the twelfth century, with the university gaining increasing prominence after the St Scholastica Day riots in 1355 when the king granted a charter that had the effect of transferring many of the powers previously held by the mayor and council, and in 1390 when Richard II gave the university's chancellor to right to hold his own court.

King Charles' decision to reinstate Oxford as the country's capital and to base himself in Christ Church has had a profound impact upon the history of all the towns and villages along the South Oxford Canal. Having held his own Parliament there, Charles was forced to flee over Port Meadow when surrounded by his enemies and although he returned he had to leave again dressed as a servant when his support began to evaporate under the threat of Cromwell's New Model Army.

Meanwhile the surrounding villages were back in survival mode. Kidlington in particular suffered badly, having taken on the role of a supplier of victuals to the king's men in Oxford, usually without any payment. The village was also the site of a couple of skirmishes in 1644 and 1645.

After the war it was decided that Oxford's castle be destroyed so the city could never become a citadel again and the period that followed saw the university gain even more powers, helped by the fact that Cromwell himself became the chancellor.

In 1718 the road from Oxford to Woodstock was turnpiked and it stayed that way for a further 160 years. It was another transport development, however, the coming of the canal, that was to herald the next significant phase in local development. Not only did this give Oxford access to coal from the Midlands (previously it had relied on fuel from the north east brought up the Thames on barges), but it opened a whole new artery into the middle of the country.

Places like Thrupp, previously a sleepy hamlet, became significant settlements, buzzing with activity. Wolvercote, the site of a paper mill owned by the Duke of Marlborough, now had direct access to coal to feed his steam engines with. As well as an academic centre, Oxford became an industrial centre.

In the twentieth century the combination of an industrial base and a reputation for free thinking and innovation led to Oxford acquiring a significant car industry due in no short measure to the efforts of William Morris, later Lord Nuffield. Although this survives in part, the area around Cowley is slowly transforming itself into a Science Park in recognition of the need to continue innovating.

The surrounding area has undergone a similar transformation. The small village of Begbroke began to grow in the 1930s, initially to house workers at the car plant, and now boasts its own hi-tech estate. Similarly, Kidlington started to build a 'garden city' to its south just before the Second World War and since then the building of other estates has transformed this 'village'. Like Oxford, Kidlington also has a Science Park and the villages along this stretch are discovering a new equilibrium with their dominant regional centre.

THE NATURAL LANDSCAPE

Two hills either side of The Wides at Enslow to the west and towards Bletchingdon to the east begin this stretch, with the Cherwell Valley, and therefore the canal also, carving a path between them. West of the valley the landscape rises again slightly at Bunkers Hill but after that flattens out onto the large open area that has been colonised by Kidlington Airport, or Oxford Airport as it prefers to be known.

The canal drops down a couple of locks the other side of Kidlington but after Duke's Lock has only one more fall before the descent into Oxford, a good demonstration of the flatness of the local landscape. This is further confirmed by the route taken by the railway and can be seen with the naked eye over Port Meadow and Wolvercote Common, which have an almost Dutch-like feel to them such is the lack of any incline, although the Burgess Field Nature Park to the east sits on a small hillock.

There are a few water meadows around, although nothing like as many as once existed on the outskirts to the city, and with the exception of Begbroke Wood, the remnants of the forests that once surrounded Oxford are conspicuous by their absence. Wolvercote is almost surrounded by water, including a large lake to the north, the Thames to the east and the canal cutting between its Upper and Lower halves. The Cherwell finally bids goodbye to the canal north of Kidlington, skirting a wide path to the east of Oxford before joining the Thames.

SECTION E

ACCESS AND TRANSPORT

ROADS

The proximity of Oxford, which most local roads as well as the canal converge into, means that this is an easy stretch to access by car. The A40 describes a line east–west across the middle of the section, cutting across the north of Oxford and provides a launch pad or intersection for a number of other main roads heading north and south.

> As it linked Oxford and Woodstock the route of the modern A44 was frequent witness to royal parties going by and there are a number of mentions in Yarnton's church records of payments to bell ringers paid to acknowledge the passage of a monarch.

The A4165 heads up from Oxford and stops just short of Kidlington, becoming the A4260, under which name it runs broadly parallel to the canal all the way to Shipton on Cherwell and then beyond to Banbury. The A34 passes to the west of Oxford and provides a link up to the M40 northeast of Kidlington, whilst its near namesake the A44 goes past Yarnton and Begbroke and then Woodstock on its way towards Evesham.

> There are five Park and Ride locations, at Pear Tree, Water Eaton, Seacourt, Thornhill and Redbridge, with buses running every 8 minutes. Details are available from 01865 785 400 or www.parkandride.net.

Local roads provide yet further access to the canal, which can be seen and reached from points as diverse as small hump-backed bridges to main arterial trunk roads. Those wishing to use their car to get into Oxford are strongly advised to use one of the Park and Ride car parks scattered around the ring road, as Oxford is not a friendly destination for motorists lacking local knowledge.

RAIL

Oxford has its own station, which picks up the Great Western Railway between Bristol and points west to London Paddington via Didcot and Reading to the east. It also acts as the terminus of the line heading north which follows the course of the canal into Banbury, as well as a link with Bicester. It is also possible to connect with cross-country services, including the south coast, from Oxford. National Train Enquiries can be reached on 08457 484950.

BUSES

Oxford is the natural focal point for bus routes in this section and as such is easily accessible by public road transport. Most local services are run by Stagecoach Oxfordshire (01865 772250) and these services are advertised in the city centre and bus station. The Oxford Bus Company (01865 785400) also provides a number of services within Oxford. Traveline (www.traveline.org.uk) on 0870 6082608 can give details of specific services between 7 a.m. and 10 p.m.

SECTION E

The main longer-distance bus operators and services linking the other communities on this stretch include:

- **Grayline Coaches** (01869 246461).
  The 3 Kidlington to Gosford circular (Mon-Fri).
  The 3a Kidlington, Begbroke and Yarnton circular (Mon-Fri).
- **Heyfordian Travel** (01869 241500).
  The 9 linking Oxford Station with Kidlington (Daily).
  The 84 linking Middle Barton, Kindlington and Oxford (Mon-Sat).
- **Kidlington Lynx** (01865 374442).
  The 1 linking Kidlington, Yarnton and Woodstock (Mon).
  The 2 linking Kidlington, Kirtlington and Weston (Mon).
  The 3 linking Kidlington, the Heyfords and Bicester (Tues).
  The 4 linking Kidlington, Bletchingdon and Bicester (Thurs).
- **RH Transport Services** (01993 868559).
  The 203 linking Bladon, Woodstock and Kidlington (Mon-Sat).
- **Thames Travel** (01491 837988).
  The 103 linking Cutteslowe, Jericho, Oxford and Wheatley (Mon-Sat).
- The **Oxford Bus Company**'s wider services include:
  The 2 linking Oxford with Kidlington (Daily).
  The 6 linking Oxford with Wolvercote (Daily).
  The x70 linking Oxford with Heathrow Airport (Daily).
  The x80 linking Oxford with Gatwick Airport (Daily).
  The x90 linking Oxford with London Victoria (Daily).
- **Stagecoach Oxfordshire**'s wider services include:
  The 7a linking Kidlington, Summertown and Oxford City Centre (Daily).
  The 100 Tube to London Victoria (Daily).

TAXIS

Companies providing taxi services along this stretch are based mainly around Kidlington and Oxford and include:

- **001 Taxis**, St Aldgates, Oxford (01865 240000).
- **Ace Cars**, Oxford (01865 420000).
- **Advance Cars**, Wolvercote (01865 316710).
- **David Roberts**, Garsington, Kidlington (01865 361722).
- **K Cars Taxi Service**, Kidlington (01865 377313).
- **Radio Taxis**, Oxford (01865 242424).
- **Sunny Cars**, Kidlington (01865 373300).

One of the many gargoyles acting as water spouts in Oxford.

SECTION E

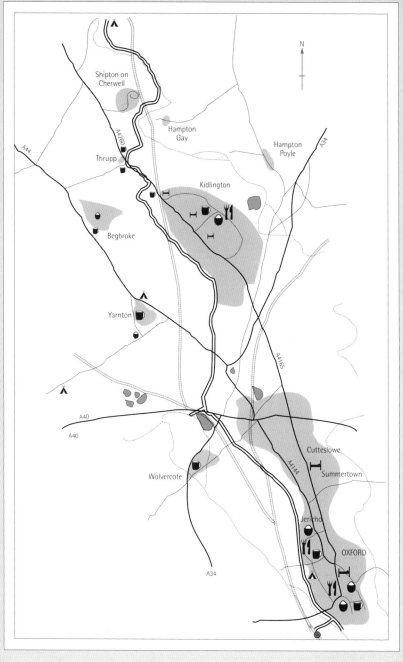

N

Shipton on
Cherwell

Hampton
Gay

Hampton
Poyle

A44

A4260

Thrupp

Kidlington

Begbroke

A34

Yarnton

A4165

A40

A40

A4144

Wolvercote

Cutteslowe

Summertown

Jericho

OXFORD

A34

Key

Canal

River

Railway

Motorway

A Road

B Road

Built up area

Stations

Open water

Shops

Accomodation

Campsite

Pub

Restaurant

NB A large symbol indicates a multiplicity of choices/options

BASICS

INTRODUCTION

Kidlington and Oxford dominate this section. Although most have pubs and some offer a little shopping or accommodation, the surrounding villages are small and lack the character seen in their Ironstone counterparts north of Banbury. As well as shops and places to stay, Oxford also has its hospitals in the Headington area of the city, slightly off the map.

SHOPPING

Those feeling starved of shopping opportunities along this canal are about to have their appetite satiated. It's no surprise that Oxford acts as a major shopping centre, although for those who don't want to brave the big city, Kidlington is also a significant location, certainly by the standards of this canal.

For those seeking more modest provisions, a Co-Op Swift Shop is signed 200yds from the Jolly Boatman in Thrupp, whilst Kidlington has a Tesco Metro and a more major Co-Op plus most banks, a pharmacy, a post office, a cycle shop and a library as well as a range of other shops.

East of the main drag of shops along Mill Street there is another small centre, the main features of which are a post office and the Cherwell Stores, offering basic provisions. Out of town to the south is a major Sainsbury's superstore.

Begbroke also has a small post office and general stores (01865 373178), which sits incongruously beneath the busy main road, whilst the Paternoster Farm Shop at the back of Yarnton (01865 372166) sells garden supplies, food including fresh vegetables and pet food. Yarnton also has a post office on the Woodstock Road (01865 372201). Wolvercote has The Post Box – as its name implies a post office – but also a general store, and has a farmers market every Sunday.

Summertown is like a small town to itself with a full range of shops, banks and post office, pharmacies and boutiques, as well of course as an Oxfam shop (the very first Oxfam shop was in Summertown), and acts as a 'taster' for Oxford itself. A lot of the big name high street names are here including Marks and Spencer and Boots and there's also a Somerfield supermarket.

Just before Oxford centre, Jericho to the north-west of the city can be quite conveniently accessed from the canal via a footbridge below Bridge 242 and is a particular haven for restaurants. Jericho retains the feel of a local community, with its convenience stores (Londis, Co-Op Swift Store), pub and café, as well as a cycle shop. There is also a good café and delicatessen, Gluttony (01865 553748).

SECTION E

The distinctive spire of Christ Church, Oxford.

The shops in Oxford itself are spread over a number of focal points. Although the pedestrianised Cornmarket Street is the most obvious centre, and indeed hosts names such as Gap, HMV, Next and WH Smith, there's also The Clarendon Centre. Shops are clustered around a number of different streets often without any kind of defining theme. Queen Street, which runs along the south and west of Cornmarket, is also free of cars, but not buses, for whom this is a major thoroughfare and Park and Ride drop-off point. This also has a number of big name stores along with the Westgate Shopping Centre at its end.

The High Street itself runs to the south and east of Cornmarket and has a number of smaller more boutique-type stores, but be wary of tourist traps as this road also takes you into one of the main college areas. St Aldgates to the south of the city also has a run of shops, including a good selection of places to grab a bite, whilst George Street to the north and west of Cornmarket has outlets of many of the most well-known restaurant chains.

At the end of George Street there is a large open space behind the bus station known as Gloucester Green where an open-air market takes place as well as a farmers' market on the first Thursday of the month from 8.30 a.m.

All in all it's probably best to resign yourself to a fair amount of foot slogging and crowd dodging when shopping in Oxford and you'll have to keep your eye open for something unexpected. This is both a working regional centre and tourist honey trap and the specialist outlets you might find in similar cities such as Bath or York seem thin on the ground.

Worthy of note outside of town are the Medley Manor Farm Pick Your Own Farm in Binsey Lane (01865 241251) and the Royal Oak Farm Shop in Beckley (01865 351246), which is just off the map to the east and sells wild and fresh meats as well as vegetables.

EATING AND DRINKING

As the character of the canal and its environs shifts from the rural to the urban so the nature of the food options available also changes. That said, the pubs which have often acted as the mainstays of eating out in previous sections should not be ignored.

The Boat (01865 374279) and Jolly Boatman (01865 377800) in Thrupp both offer good restaurant dining, whilst the Bell in Hampton Poyle (01865 848582) is also worth a visit. The Wise Alderman (01865 372281) just into Kidlington, whilst less grand than the nearby pubs in Thrupp, also does a mean pub meal and has a large car park and children's play area.

Other pubs in Kidlington, most of which offer food also, include:

- **The Squire Bassett** (01865 373107) on the Oxford Road.
- **The Black Horse** (01865 373154), on the Banbury Road near the entrance to the shops.
- **The Six Bells** (01865 373107) – a local in the heart of old Kidlington.
- **The Red Lion** (01865 373435) – a large town pub on the main road.
- **The King's Arms**, (01865 373004) in the heart of the old village.

Elsewhere in Kidlington there is a selection of takeaways and restaurants with the accent firmly on fish and chips and eastern dining. The Rainbow (01865 372603) in the main parade of shops serves just the first of these, whilst The Star on the Banbury Road (01865 372129) offers both fish and chips and Chinese. The Tandoori Nights Dial a Curry Service (01865 847755) offers free delivery within a 7-mile radius, with Tiffins Indian Takeaway (01865 372245) offering an alternative.

If you want more of a restaurant experience your best bet is probably Ovishers Tandoori (01865 372827), also on the Banbury Road, whilst if

The delightful Trout Inn, Wolvercote, by the river.

it's a light bite you're after, try Sami's Coffee Shop on the Banbury Road (01865 848088), which sells a selection of pizzas, burgers and baguettes as well as coffee of course.

Outside of Kidlington there's the The Royal Sun in Begbroke (01865 372231) and The Turnpike (01865 847666), the Red Lion (01865 373556) and The Grapes (01865 372120) all in Yarnton.

> The Turnpike in Yarnton was recently renamed in acknowledgement of the pub's origins as the original turnpike, a pre-industrial toll road, was established here in 1718.

Heading into Wolvercote there is a choice of four pubs; the Red Lion, (01865 552722); The White Hart (01865 554080); The Plough on the Green (01865 556969) and of course The Trout Inn (01865 302171) out towards Godstow Priory on the river, which is a definite gastro-pub experience. There's also a Chinese takeaway and fish and chip shop near the first two of these pubs, the Dak Bo (01865 310439).

Entering Oxford from a slightly more easterly direction you will come through Summertown, whose pubs includce The Dew Drop Inn (01865 559372) and the Anchor (01865 510282). Places to eat in Summertown include Mama Mia Pizzeria (01865 514141) and La Dolce Vita (01865 553990), as well as the Blue Palms Brasserie (01865 559653), which has a Mediterranean/Moroccan feel to it. Approach Oxford from the A4144 and you will pass The Woodstock Arms (01865 552454), which also serves food.

Whilst you will definitely not starve in Oxford you may equally struggle to find a meal to remember. Given the high proportion of students it's understandable that there are a good variety of 'cheap eats', ranging from falafel to noodles through pizzas, tapas and baguettes. The city's role as a tourist destination also means that there are a lot of well-known high street names where familiarity may win out over adventurousness.

If you do want something a little different you might be best advised to wander up to Jericho and browse the various menus along Walton Street, including Le Petit Blanc, owned by the famous chef Raymond Blanc (01865 510999).

The following selections of light bites, fast food and takeaways are just that, a selection offered as a starter for the uninitiated, and you're best advised to wander and try for yourself:

Oxford lunchers, spied from above.

- **Cock and Camel Café**, George Street (01865 203705) – *a lively continental-style café bar.*
- **Eurobar Café**, George Street (01865 725057).
- **George and Danver**, St Aldgates and Little Clarendon Street (01865 516652) – *ice cream, sandwiches and coffee as well as good vegetarian options.*
- **Harvey's Sandwich Bars**, Gloucester Green and High Street (01865 793963).
- **La Tapas Spanish Bar**, Little Clarenden Street (01865 516688).
- **Jericho Café**, Walton Street, Jericho (01865 310840).
- **Sang Hing House**, Walton Street, Jericho (01865 553455) – *Chinese cuisine.*

More formal dining possibilities away from the big chains include the following:

- **Bistro Je T'Aime**, Blue Boar Street (01865 722474) – *French.*
- **The Chang Mai**, High Street (01865 202233) – *Thai.*
- **Jamal's Tandoori**, Walton Street, Jericho (01865 554405).
- **Loch Fyne**, Jericho (01865 292510) – *specialising in fish.*
- **Opium Den**, Worcester Street (01865 248680) – *Chinese.*
- **The Pink Giraffe**, St Clements (01865 202787) – *vegetarian and seafood.*
- **Restaurant du Liban**, Broad Street (01865 242494) – *Lebanese.*

Given Oxford's history and its role as a centre of student life it should come as no surprise that there is no shortage of watering holes. These vary from small hole-in-the-wall affairs with a history spanning centuries through to more modern bars, although thankfully Oxford, in its centre at least, seems to have avoided the curse of the big town pub.

It's perfectly possible to construct a pub crawl of your own taking in literary associations or to simply take pot luck on the basis of what a pub looks like from the outside. Some are on the main roads linking the city's different quarters, whilst other more interesting affairs exist down some of the alleyways, most notably to the south of the High Street.

As with advice on eating, the following list offers a selection of pubs you may wish to visit:

- **Antiquity Hall**, Hythe Bridge Street (01865 249153) – *near the canal terminus, a popular venue for live music.*
- **The Bear** (01865 721783), junction of Blue Boar and Alfred Streets – *one of Oxford's oldest buildings tucked away down an alley. Famous for its collection of signed and dated neckties.*
- **The Eagle and Child**, St Giles (01865 310154) – *an inn since 1650, known locally as the Bird and Baby. A favourite of both C.S. Lewis and J.R.R. Tolkein.*
- **The Head of the River**, Folly Bridge (01865 721600) – *a large pub overlooking the Thames.*
- **The Jericho Tavern**, Walton Street (01865 311775) – *the pub the Jericho area is named after.*
- **The Kings Arms**, Holywell Street (01865 242369) – *near the Sheldonian, originally a religious site owned by Augustian friars.*
- **Next Door**, Holywell Street (01865 203536) – *a listed building despite only being completed in 1972. Good food and a pomegranate tree in the middle.*
- **The Old Tom**, St Aldgates (01865 243034) – *popular with students from Christ Church but small and therefore can become crowded.*
- **The Turf**, Bath Place off Holywell Street (01865 243235) – *another pub down an alley with an enclosed beer garden, hard to find but worth it when you get there!*

SLEEPING

For such a major destination, Oxford has traditionally suffered from a shortage of hotel accommodation, although this is now beginning to change. For this reason many of the tourists who visit the city come only for the day. Round and about there is the usual mixture of B&Bs and guesthouses, with a liberal sprinkling of these in the Summertown area north of Oxford also. The following list offers a selection:

HOTELS
- **Bath Place Hotel**, Bath Place, Oxford (01865 791812).
- **Bowood House Hotel**, Kidlington (01865 842288).
- **Cock and Camel Hotel**, George Street, Oxford (01865 203705).
- **Galaxie Hotel**, Summertown, Oxford (01865 515688).

- **Linton Lodge Hotel**, Linton Road (01865 553461).
- **Marlborough House Hotel**, Woodstock Road (01865 311321).
- **Old Bank Hotel**, High Street, Oxford (01865 799599).
- **Parklands Hotel**, Summertown (01865 554374).

- **The River Hotel**, Botley Road, Oxford (01865 243475).
- **Royal Oxford Hotel**, Park End Street, Oxford (01865 248432).
- **Tower House**, Ship Street, Oxford (01865 246828).

BED AND BREAKFASTS/GUESTHOUSES

- **Adams Guest House**, Summertown (01865 565118).
- **The Bear**, Alfred Street, Oxford (01865 728164).
- **Chestnuts Guest House**, Woodstock Road, Oxford (01865 553375).
- **College Guest House**, Woodstock Road, Oxford (01865 552579).
- **Cotswold House Guest House**, Summertown (01865 310558).
- **Eltham Villa Guest House**, Yarnton (01865 376037).
- **Five Mile View Guest House**, Banbury Road, Oxford (01865 558747).

- **Greenhill Farm**, Kidlington (01865 350271).
- **Lonsdale Guest House**, Summertown (01865 554872).
- **Number Two**, Turnpike Cottages, Kidlington (01869 350706).
- **Park House**, St Bernards Road, Oxford (01865 310824).
- **The Turf**, Bath Place off Holywell Street (01865 243235).
- **Warsborough House** (B&B) Kidlington (01865 370316).

You may also wish to consider self-catering if you intend to stay a while. If so, the following contacts offer a starting point:

- Apartments in Oxford (01865 254000).
- Thackley End (01865 557555).

CAMPING

Camping sites along this stretch include:

- **Salter Brothers**, The Slipway, Donnington Bridge, Oxford (01865 243421).
- **Cassington Mill Caravan Park**, Cassington near Yarnton (01865 881081).

- **Lince Copse Caravan and Camping Park** (01869 331508).
- **Swinford Farm Camping and Caravan Site**, near Yarnton (01865 881368).

SECTION E

Key

Canal	Built up area	Site/Sight
River	Stations	Leisure
Railway	Open water	Entertainment
Motorway		Culture
A Road		
B Road		

NB A large symbol indicates a multiplicity of choices/options

Shipton on Cherwell
Hampton Gay
Hampton Poyle
Thrupp
Kidlington
Begbroke
Yarnton
Cutteslowe
Summertown
Wolvercote
Jericho
OXFORD
A44
A4260
A34
A40
A40
A34
A4165
A4144
N

SEEING AND DOING

INTRODUCTION

Understandably Oxford tends to dominate the attention when it comes to seeing and doing along this section. It would be a mistake to home in on Oxford alone however. The city's Jericho near-suburb and the village of Wolvercote slightly to the north alone provide sights worth visiting, whilst the surrounding villages, including Kidlington, all have their own history. Yarnton's church in particular is an often-missed gem.

There are two Tourist Information Centres along this stretch. The one in Kidlington (01865 378479) is well hidden behind a high hedge in the Exeter Hall complex opposite the library, whilst the one in Oxford (01865 726871) is more prominent, although again rather tucked away to the north of the city.

SIGHTS

The Manor House in Shipton has belonged to the entrepreneur Richard Branson who renovated it and converted some of the outbuildings into recording studios. Hampton Gay, which can be reached by footpath east of Shipton or via a track to the east, is the site of an abandoned village, the remains of which can be made out as raised plots in the fields, although a church still remains. This was once the site of a paper mill supplying the university, which before being converted to this use operated as a corn mill.

There were once plans to cut a canal from Hampton Gay to provide an alternative route to the Thames at Isleworth via Thame, Wendover and Amersham. Although surveyed twice, and despite support from both the Oxford and the Thames and Severn canal companies, the plans never came to fruition.

The railway runs to the west of here and was the scene of the worst disaster experienced by the Great Western Railway when, on Christmas Eve 1874 the 10 a.m. express from London to Birkenhead crashed when one of the carriage's wheels came loose and the driver braked too hard. Nine carriages tumbled into the canal leading to the deaths of thirty-four people, including two children.

From 1932-37 Kidlington was the site of Oxford Zoo. During the Second World War the same site was used by evacuated pupils from East Ham Girl's Grammar School. The conversion from zoo to school was done in a hurry and it is said that the girls were taught in rooms with signs warning that 'These Animals May be Dangerous'!

Thrupp is best visited when the sun is out and the mood is sleepy. The cottages that line the canal were originally salt warehouses and

SECTION E

although now called Boat Row this line of houses was originally called Salt Row. The old Baptist church was sold in 1953 to help start a church in Kidlington, whilst in the late nineteenth century the licensee of the Jolly Boatman pub, then known as the Britannia, was also a blacksmith and a coal merchant. The Boat Inn down the path was similarly entrepreneurial, with the pub also operating as a grocers shop.

Despite its outwardly modern appearance it is worth pausing a while in Kidlington and scratching the surface to see what's underneath as really it's a village of two parts. The community's history stretches back to Roman times when the Portway Road passed down what is now Church Street before joining Akeman Street.

Thomas Beecham, he of the powders, lived briefly in Kidlington when he was in his early twenties. He lived with his uncle, a shepherd, in a house that came to be known as Pill Cottage as it was from the grass behind the cottage that he discovered the formula for one of his pills. Fame and fortune were to follow later however and during his time in Kidlington he made his living as a postman and jobbing gardener.

The church of St Mary the Virgin was built in 1220 and is noted for its medieval glass and ancient misericords and bench ends. The slender spire of the church is known as 'Our Lady's Needle'. This and other historical sights are tucked away down Church Street and Mill Street at the end of the road heading away from the shops.

Mr Georges' Room, Kidlington Almshouse.

These include the almshouses built by Sir William Morton, the Royalist commander of Studeley Castle, as part of his will on land to the east of the church. These were established 'for the habitation and maintenance of three poore men and three poore women that are impotent and decrepit, who are single persons and whose labour and worke is done'. The upper three rooms were dedicated to his wife and two daughters and the lower three to his three sons, whose names are still visible today in inscriptions over the windows. Quite how kindly they took to being forever associated with the impotent and decrepit is not recorded.

Other buildings worth looking out for include the Dovecote near the old Rectory, which can be dated back to 1290 and has 400 holes in thirteen rows, Hampden Manor off Mill Street, and Burnt Oak further down Mill Street, a late seventeenth-century former farm house where French prisoners were held during the Napoleonic Wars. A useful way to see these and other sites is to follow the Kidlington Historic Village Trail, copies of which can be obtained from the Tourist Centre.

Kidlington Airport was founded in 1938 and was later leased to General Aircraft Ltd for civil use. The Air Ministry requisitioned it during the war and set up a flying school. These days it is one of the country's main pilot training schools, so don't assume that the low flying craft around you are under control! Since opening in 1962 the modern school has trained over 10,000 pilots for eighty airlines from forty different countries.

Just south of Kidlington is Stratford Brake, 45 acres owned by the Woodland Trust where there's an information board telling you what to look out for. Yarnton church is well worth a detour. Well signposted and sitting on the edge of the village near the Manor House, there's a cross in the churchyard, one of four that once acted as pilgrimage points for the local Abbot and his monks in the Middle Ages, but it's when you go inside that the splendour of the place hits you. A side chapel devoted to the Spencer family, built by Sir Thomas of that ilk in 1611 at a time when he was altering the whole structure of the twelfth-century fabric, has an amazing red and gold roof as well as a memorial more suited to a church in Florence or Rome.

> Sir Thomas Spencer also gave the church a peal of six bells, only one of which has ever had to be replaced.

The Spencer Memorial in Yarnton's church.

Cutteslowe is best known for its park, which was acquired by the local council in stages during the 1930s. There's a large ornamental pond, a miniature railway, which runs every other Sunday during the summer, gardens and a paddling pool, as well as a very large children's play area.

Lower Wolvercote sits on Port Meadow, at the top of which lies the ruins of the fourteenth-century Bendictine Godstow Abbey where Henry II's mistress Rosamund the Fair was imprisoned and is still said to haunt the site. Passing into private ownership after the dissolution of the monasteries, the house was severely damaged during the Civil War.

Just over the bridge lies the Trout Inn, destined from now on to be forever associated with *Inspector Morse*, although its popularity predates the grumpy policeman. Originally Godstow House, the building also suffered from the attentions of the competing armies during the Civil War. Look into the water near the weir and admire the gigantic fish that play there.

Continue up the road from the river and on the left after another bridge is a memorial to two early officers of the Royal Flying Corps who ditched their experimental monoplane a hundred yards from the

SECTION E

bridge in 1912, a subsequent public subscription raising the money for the tablet.

Further up is a public car park behind where, in the field behind it, a metal marker defines the 1860 city limit. This is not the original though, this being a stone marker that now sits in the drive of the thatched cottage at No.182 behind.

Summertown was created in 1820 when a local baker divided his field into building lots. It officially became part of Oxford in 1889 when its drains and sewers were connected to the city's system. Summertown was the birthplace of Oxfam, Oxford Famine Relief, with offices above the first ever shop until recently still occupied by the charity as part of its sprawling headquarters. Over the road is BBC Radio Oxford.

Residents of Wolvercote are known as commoners and have the right to graze their horses on Port Meadow and horses are still rounded up annually to exercise this right. Wolvercote also has a community orchard, established in 1994 on land owned by the Oxfordshire Preservation Trust. The aim of the orchard is to propogate and preserve old varieties of Oxfordshire apple. There is an Apple Day every October, during which some of the thirty types of apple grown here can be tasted, alongside pear, quince, cherries and plums.

Finally in this surprising place there is Wolvercote Cemetery which has won national awards and includes a number of sections for different nationalities and faiths. J.R.R. Tolkein is buried in the Catholic area.

Oxford's near-suburb of Jericho is a residential area of Victorian terraced houses that retains a community feel to it and is a great place just to wander if you want to escape Oxford's centre for a while. It's only a few minutes walk north and there's a circular route back via the canal.

Much of the building was thrown up in a hurry and some say that Jericho's name is derived from 'jerry-building' or the Biblical story about the walls coming tumbling down. In Hardy's *Jude The Obscure* the area is recorded as a slum, possibly due to the nearby Lucy's Ironworks, which employed many of the local residents.

The real origin of the area's name probably roots back to the Jericho tavern which dates back to 1650 – or possibly because the area was built on an area known as Jericho Gardens. Jericho is home to the world-famous Oxford University Press, which has been here since 1826 and has traditionally employed many of the workers housed in the 'two-up two-down' terraces that line the streets. The houses down Kingston Road with their Gothic doorways and mock half-timbering are particularly worth a look.

Oxford is an experience as much as a location; there is no single sight to home in on like the Royal Crescent or Pump Rooms in Bath. The dispersed nature of the colleges means that places to visit or simply see are similarly spread out.

The visitor has a number of options to counter this. Either they can take advantage of one of the tours, by bus or on foot, detailed in the Sampling section, or visit the Oxford Story (see below) to gain a historical perspective. Alternatively they can climb up to one of the vantage points such as the Carfax Tower at the junction of Queen and High Streets with Cornmarket Street or the church towers of St Mary the Virgin or St Michael, to gain a visual perspective.

The colleges vary in the warmth with which they welcome visitors, understandably perhaps given that they exist as places of learning and nothing puts you off studying more than being gawped at or being photographed. Those that do and have the most hospitable arrangements for tourists include Christ Church (01865 276492, charge) largely due to the fact that the Cathedral is also a Diocesan centre, Balliol (01865 277777 small charge, afternoons only), Corpus Christi (01865 276700, afternoons only, free), Hertford near the Bridge of Sighs opposite the Sheldonian (01865 279400, free) and St Johns, where Tony Blair studied (01865 277300). This is only a selection though with many more opening their doors; see 'Learn More and Links' for further details.

> At 1,000 years old the Saxon tower of St Michael's church is thought to be the oldest surviving building in Oxford.

> Hertford's Bridge of Sighs is a nineteenth-century copy of the Venetian original. Hertford was also the setting for Evelyn Waugh's classic of Oxford life *Brideshead Revisited*.

Simply wandering around on foot reveals a number of wonders, with highlights including the Sheldonian Theatre and the Radcliffe Camera. The Sheldonian often hosts concerts (see Culture below) whilst the Radcliffe Camera acts as the Bodelian Library's Reading Room and was built between 1737 and 1749 by James Gibb. Nearby is the site of Blackwells, or rather one of them, the famous booksellers.

The Ashmolean Museum in Beaumont Street (01865 278000) is free and houses one of the finest collections of art and antiquities in the country, if not the world. The collections cover both Western and Eastern art as well as coins and casts as well as antiquities from the ancient world.

> Hidden away in an upper room of the Ashmolean are the remnants of the royal gardener John Trudescant's collection of curiosities, widely felt to be the first ever museum in the modern sense.

The Museum of Oxford (01865 52761) at the corner of Blue Boar Street and St Aldgates does what it says on the can, namely it covers the history of Oxford from prehistoric times, whilst the Oxford Museum of Natural History on Parks Road (01865 270927) also delivers what it promises in its title and claims to have *Alice in Wonderland*'s rabbit (stuffed of course).

Through this museum is the Pitt Rivers Museum, which bucks the trend by being something completely different than its name would suggest, namely an ethnographic and archaeological collection focusing on items from the Pacific Islands. Finally, the Museum of the History of Science on Broad Street (01865 277080) in the old Ashmolean building, houses a fascinating collection of the scientific instruments tracing the development of scientific thought.

CULTURE

Oxford's reputation as a cultural centre goes before it and is justified, although at times in the recent past it would have been difficult to agree if you'd stood before the billboards of the Apollo Theatre in George Street. Now renamed the New Theatre (0870 6063500) Oxford's largest theatre has to fill seats to survive and the programme here can vary from opera to *Singalong-a-Elvis*, with the venue also popular with touring artists and houses.

The smaller Oxford Playhouse (01865 305305) tends to aim at the more refined end of the spectrum, but can bring itself to stage the occasional musical as well as Shakespeare and Chekov. The theatre's studio, the Burton Taylor Theatre (same number) offers more contemporary offerings. The Pegasus Theatre (01865 792209), on Magdalen Road slightly off the map, is the home of Oxford Youth Theatre and offers a varied programme.

Oxford also has a tradition of open-air performance and it is worth checking the Tourist Information Centre to see if there's anything on, for example in the Sheldonian Theatre courtyard, where Shakespeare is a favourite. Cutteslowe Park also has the occasional concert, sometimes featuring international stars.

Music is another Oxford speciality, with the Sheldonian a popular venue again along with the Holywell Room (07976 039385). The city has its own recently formed professional Symphony Orchestra, the Philomusica (0870 305305), which also has the Sheldonian as its preferred venue. The Oxford Folk Club offers a more prosaic sound at the Port Mahon in St Clements every Friday night (01865 768128). Finally, if you get the chance try and listen to the Christ Church Choir in the Cathedral.

It is also worth pausing to consider some of the art available to view in Oxford both at the Museum of Modern Art, St Aldgates (01865 813830) and the Christ Church Picture Gallery, which is accessed via Oriel Square (01865 276150) and houses over 300 old masters and 2,000 drawings with an emphasis on Italian art from the fourteenth to eighteenth centuries.

Finally, the Old Fire Station in George Street (01865 297170) stages a range of drama and other entertainment.

ENTERTAINMENT

This section is a good place to be if you're feeling starved of sporting opportunities, either as participant or spectator. The Kidlington and Gosford Sports Centre (01865 376368), run by Cherwell District Council, has a full range of health and fitness facilities as well as badminton and squash courts, Astroturf, a crèche and 25m pool.

Equally, the Ferry Sports Centre, Summertown (01865 467060) has a pool along with the usual gym and spa-type facilities. Off the map, there are further opportunities for swimming at the Temple Cowley indoor pool (01865 467110) and the Hinksey park outdoor complex (01865 467079) on the Abingdon Road.

Oxford also has its own Ice Rink (01865 467000) within easy reach of the city centre and regular athletics meetings are held at the University's Iffley Road Track (01865 240476) where the four-minute mile was first broken. Kidlington also has an athletics club (01865 460269).

Oxford has its own professional football team, Oxford United, which now plays in the modern Kassam Stadium (01865 337500) out of town on the ring road, and first class cricket is played at the university's Parks Road ground (01865 557106) from April to July. Further down the leagues, Kidlington also has a cricket team (01865 377277).

If the weather is fine it seems a shame not to enjoy the river. The lazy way is to take a boat trip using Salters Steamers (01865 243421), who offer return trips to Abingdon or, if time is short, to Iffley lock and back (40 minutes) from May to September starting from Folly Bridge. The harder, but perhaps more traditional option, is punting. Three places offer this; Folly Bridge again (0961 115369); Magdalen Bridge (01865 761586) and the Cherwell Boathouse (01865 515978).

There are four cinemas in Oxford; two Odeons, one near St Giles and one in George Street (both 0870 5050007); the Pheonix Picture House in Jericho (01865 512 526) and the Ultimate Picture Palace (UPP) (01865 245288) in Jeune Street off the map. Although listed under entertainment rather than culture, the latter two are independent with the UPP in particular showing a selection of 'art house' and foreign films.

On this subject, a trip to the Tourist Information Centre will yield a harvest of possible options within Oxford, with a fine line existing between sightseeing, cultural nourishment and good old fashioned entertainment. One attraction that probably combines all three is The Oxford Story (01865 728822), located conveniently close to the Centre. This is a 25-minute 'dark ride' on an electrically driven car tracing Oxford's history and achievements. Sights, sounds and smells are provided and this can be a useful introduction to the city for visitors of any age.

Two other attractions worth mentioning from the many available are Alice's Shop, famous as the inspiration for Lewis Carroll's 'Sheep Shop' in *Alice Through The Looking Glass*, and the Botanical Gardens. The shop sells Alice merchandise and can arrange for Alice Tours of the City, where Carroll wrote and lived (01865 723793). The Botanical Gardens (01865 286690) describe themselves as a living library and offer a sanctuary of calm within easy reach of the centre of the city.

Outside of Oxford other than the sports centres entertainment tends to be locally driven. Yarnton has a very impressive set of children's play equipment and Begbroke a Sports and Social Club with a strong bowls section (01865 373536).

SECTION E

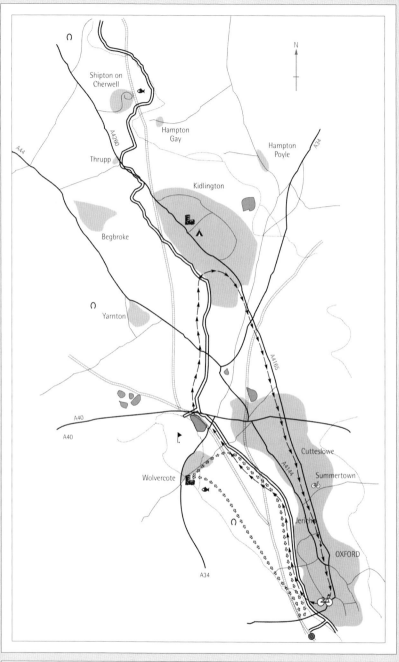

N

Shipton on
Cherwell

Hampton
Gay

Hampton
Poyle

Thrupp

A44

A4260

A34

Kidlington

Begbroke

Yarnton

A40

A40

A4185

A4165

A4144

Cutteslowe

Summertown

Wolvercote

Jericho

OXFORD

A34

Key

━━━━ Canal
·········· River
▥▥▥ Railway
─ ─ ─ Motorway
──── A Road
──── B Road

⬤ Built up area
🔵 Stations
🔵 Open water

🚲➜ Cycling route/outlet
👢⇨ Walking route/outlet
🐟 Fishing spot/outlet

Ω Riding outlet
⚑ Golf course/outlet

NB A large symbol indicates a multiplicity of choices/options

SAMPLING

INTRODUCTION

Good transport links mean it is easy to sample what this section has to offer. Ironically perhaps, whereas the canal has been one of the main arteries through the previous sections, after Kidlington it tends to become fairly anonymous here, and almost creeps into Oxford unannounced.

With the alternative route into the Thames at Duke's Cut many boaters choose to avoid this stretch. This is a shame, for although the urban nature of this run is out of character with much of the rest of the canal, it is worth seeing, and this is reflected in both the cycle route and walk offered here.

Sampling Oxford itself is a different business. Doing so by car is not advised, and its dispersed nature means that doing so by foot can become a tiring and at times confusing business; although ultimately this is probably the best way of doing it. If you're in a hurry one

> Hop On-Hop Off buses are run by City Sightseeing Oxford (01865 790522) and Full Circle Tours (01789 720002).

of the open top buses, complete with running commentary, or one of the Guided Walks from the Tourist Information Centre are both good options.

WALKING

Despite a fair smattering of footpaths this is not the best of stretches for solo walking, with parts of the canal towpath featuring in most circular walks largely through necessity. It is possible to turn this to your advantage, with Kidlington having its own town trail and a number of under-appreciated footways through Oxford itself.

If you want to 'go it alone' you can either use the Thames Path, which tends to be well signed, or follow one of the walks around the underbelly of the city. One of these starts at the entrance to Christ Church Meadow off St Aldgates. Either follow this along the Broad Walk to the Cherwell and then head left (north) to the Botanic Gardens, or take the path on the right opposite the entrance to the Cathedral, The New Walk, although newness is relative in Oxford, towards the Thames. An alternative is to head left after the Cathedral and turn right after 100yds or so along Dead Man's Walk, again towards the Botanical Gardens.

If you want to explore the colleges and history of the city with an experienced guide there are a number of timed and guided walks (01865 726871) all of which start from the Tourist Information Centre in Broad Street. You may need to book a slot and come back. There's even an *Inspector Morse* walk and Ghost Tours Friday and Saturday nights – and Hallow'een of course.

Walk E takes in both the towpath and a portion of the Thames, sandwiched in the middle by a brief exposure to the bustle of the city around its station. Wolvercote is well worth exploring and should not simply be used as a convenient place to leave the car!

SECTION E WALK

From Upper Wolvercote and Back via Canal Terminus

Description:	*An opportunity to sample both canal and the River Thames via Oxford's empty west side, taking in a nature reserve.*
Distance:	*7 miles*
Duration:	*3hrs*
Staring point:	*Grid Reference 487095, OS Explorer 180 (W)*
Nearest Refreshment:	*Any of three pubs in Upper Wolvercote*

Start in the public car park facing Port Meadow on the way to The Trout Inn. Turn right out of the car park and head up the road, along the track and past the post office. Cross over the first of two bridges and pick up the canal towpath just before the second, heading right or south. From here simply stick with the towpath through its lengthy conservation area and past the various long-term moorings until you reach Oxford.

The canal's effective end is marked by Isis Lock and a black and white iron bridge. Just before this, the path diverges to the right over a footbridge. Take this and emerge into some modern housing. Follow this round, taking the first right and then right again at the top onto a foot and cycleway round to the station. Cross in front of this and pick up the pavement along the main road, heading right. On reaching Osney Bridge by the River Hotel take the Thames Path on the right and follow this past a row of cottages.

Cross over another iron bridge and continue alongside the river until you reach a marina. Here you take the wooden plank bridge on your right and enter the meadow. Aim half left, skirting some wetland, and pick up an unmade road which brings you to the Burgess Field Nature Park. Here you can either enter the park or stick with the meadow. Either way, your target is Wolvercote due north, which although it seems a long way away is less than 1.5 miles distant.

On nearing Wolvercote aim for the row of seven white cottages and on reaching them turn left onto the road and head back to your starting point on familiar territory.

Outlets selling walking equipment supplies along this stretch include:

- **Blacks**, St Aldgates, Oxford (01865 727632).
- **Camping and Outdoor Centre**, Turl Street, Oxford (01865 247110).
- **Field and Trek**, St Clements Street, Oxford (01865 247948).
- **Millets, Queen Street**, Oxford (01865 790676).
- **Two Degrees West**, Clarendon Street, Oxford (01865 310544).

RIDING

As first Kidlington and then Oxford begin to exert their presence so the opportunities for riding fall away as the canal finally reaches its destination. Whilst some bridleways do exist they tend to take the rider out of the mapped area and towards the surrounding countryside. One such path heads west from the A4095 just west of Enslow Bridge before linking up with Samson's Lane running north–south to the east of Woodstock.

Another path links Bladon with Yarnton, joining the latter just north of the village on the Woodstock Road (Dolton Lane) and it is also possible to ride down to the Thames from Mead Farm just to the south of Yarnton along a public bridleway. Just south of Gosford Bridge on the eastern outskirts of Kidlington there's another path that zig-zags across fields in a vague easterly direction before joining a further path that heads north towards the Cherwell at Islip and south and then west towards the Oxford Road just north of Cuttleslowe.

Finally, the path cutting across Port Meadow south of Wolvercote, featured in Walk E, is also a public bridleway, offering the opportunity to take in the large open space between the canal and the Thames that offers a quiet sanctuary before the city.

Riding establishments along this stretch include:

- **G.J. Brown & Sons**, Woodeaton, Oxford (01865 559685).
- **Long Leys Riding Centre and Stud**, Cumnor, just off the south-
- west corner of the map (01865 864554).
- **Old Manor House Riding School**, Botley, Oxford (01865 242274).

CYCLING

Oxford is famous for its bikes, with tradition demanding that every student buy and use a cycle to get around. Although the reality is less romantic, bikes proliferate around the city and the local council is keen to promote their use (see 'Learn More and Links').

The well-signed Oxfordshire Cycleway offers a circular ride around the county and National Cycleway Routes 5 and 15 both go through Oxford, with the first of these following the canal towpath before picking up the A44 to Woodstock. A three-way marker at Duke's Cut

SECTION E

on the canal directs the cyclist either towards the Thames, Oxford or points north.

As you might expect, the canal towpath itself is in generally good condition for cycling, being firm and free of overhanging vegetation. A recommended route starts appropriately enough at the canal's end near the Hythe Street car park, appropriate because this was the site of the original canal basin, which there are plans to resurrect.

Head north, passing Jericho on your right and then the open grounds of Port Meadow on your left. Continue past Duke's Cut before heading due north towards the outskirts of Kidlington. Leave the canal at Bridge 228 (Yarnton Bridge) and head left (west) along Sandy Lane into Yarnton. Just after the garden centre head right, or north, along the A44 to Begbroke and beyond before turning right at the side road signposted to the airport, although the sight of lots of planes overhead should make this obvious.

Head along this road into Kidlington and if you have time take a detour into Thrupp at the T-junction by picking up the towpath at the Wise Alderman and heading left. On returning head through Kidlington, past the Garden City, to the large superstore roundabout. Here you need to head straight over, but it is very busy here so take care. You are now on the old Oxford Road which takes you into Summertown via another roundabout (again, go straight over).

This route allows you to experience a typical student's – or more likely cycling don's – commuter route into the heart of Oxford. Stick with this road until you reach the Randolph Hotel, where you turn right past the Ashmolean and then left back to your starting point. This combination of canal, surrounding towns and villages and city centre adds up to around 16 miles' cycling.

Cycle supplies are plentiful and include the following:

- **Bee-Line Bicycles**, Cowley Road, Oxford (01865 246615).
- **Bicycles**, Woodstock Road, Summertown, Oxford (01865 514584).
- **Bike Zone**, Market Street, Oxford (01865 728877).
- **Cycle King**, Cowley Road, Oxford (01865 728262).
- **Cyclo Analysts**, Cowley Road, Oxford (01865 424444).
- **GR Cycles**, Kidlington (01865 374588).
- **Halfords**, Between Towns Road, Oxford (01865 749494).
- **Smith and Low**, Hollow Way, Oxford (01865 777946).
- **Reg Taylor**, Iffley Road, Oxford (01865 247040).
- **Walton Street Cycles**, Oxford (01865 310625).

FISHING

Not only is fishing available along the canal, but the Cherwell and even the Thames, as well as a number of lakes surrounding this stretch all offer good pitches. The following is a guide to some of the better places to fish, but is far from a comprehensive listing and anglers are advised to test the local waters for themselves:

- **The River Cherwell at Shipton on Cherwell** *is a good stretch with a backwater and a weir pool offering barbell up to 11lb (near the weir pool), chub up to 5lb (near the railway bridge) and bream up to 7lb as well as tench, perch (near the cattle ramp), roach, grayling and dace (controlled by the Banbury and District AA).*
- **The Oxford Canal at Thrupp** *offers good bream and carp, with the former found at the turning point. Further upstream where the rushes* line the bank tench and carp can be fished, along with some large carp (controlled by the Thrupp Mooring Association).*
- **The River Thames at Wolvercote,** *a 0.75-mile stretch of tree lined river, both sides of which can be fished. Good for perch with roach, chub and bream up to 5lb and pike up to 15lb, with live baits acceptable when fishing for the latter (controlled by the North Oxford AS).*

Other good fishing spots in these parts include Duke's Lake and Pickford Lake near Oxford (01865 79582), which are both good for carp, and Blenheim Palace Lake in Woodstock (01993 811432) which has mainly tench and bream with the occasional pike up to 20lb which can be fished from punts, although you will need to pre-arrange a spot first.

Fishing supplies can be obtained from:

- Fat Phil's Angling Centre, Abingdon Road, Oxford (01865 201020).
- The Predator Angling Centre, Kidlington (01865 372066).

OTHER

Golf courses and equipment suppliers in the area covered by and close to this stretch include:

- **Studley Wood Golf Club,** Horton cum Studley, about 4 miles north-east of Oxford (01865 351122) – *18 holes, 6811yds.*
- **Hinksey Heights Golf Club,** Hinksey, about 2 miles south of Oxford (01865 327775) – *18 holes, 6936yds plus a 9-hole par three course.*
- **Ultimate Golf,** Between Towns Road, Oxford (01865 715217) – *golf shop.*
- **Southfield Golf Club,** near the Headington Hospitals (01865 242158) – *18 holes, 6328yds.*
- **North Oxford Golf Club,** Wolvercote (01865 554415) – *18 holes, 5736yds.*
- **Waterstock Golf Club,** near Junction 8a of the M40 (01865 338093) – *18 holes, 6535yds.*

SECTION E

LEARN MORE AND LINKS

For those wishing to delve a little further into the places and events covered in this guide, the following list, whilst far from comprehensive, should act as a useful starting point:

Tourist Information

Banbury Tourist Information Centre (01295 259855).

Cherwell District Council – offers a number of leaflets and a range of information for downloading on its website: www.cherwell-dc.gov.uk. Also available by post from the Leisure Services Department (01295 221706).

Kidlington Tourist Information Centre (01869 369055).

www.visitnorthoxfordshire.co.uk – tourism site covering the whole of North Oxfordshire run by Cherwell District Council.

Websites offering information on specific places or events:

www.3parishes.co.uk – Souldern
www.adderbury.net – Adderbury
www.banbury-cross.co.uk
www.banburytown.co.uk
www.banbury-web.co.uk – directory of businesses and activities in North Oxfordshire and Banbury area.
www.deddington.org.uk – Deddington.
www.deddington.org.uk/history/ countryside/countryside3.html – further details on Deddington Castle including an overview of the site, a little bit of history about the castle and details of the local countryside.
www.faircrop.co.uk – details on the annual Cropredy Fesitval.
www.oxtowns.co.uk/banbury
www.rideacockhorse.co.uk – for more on the folk club performing in The Mill in Banbury every Wednesday evening.
www.thisisoxfordshire.co.uk/ oxfordshire/visit/colleges-html – Oxford college viewing arrangements.

Book offering further detail on specific places or aspects of local history:

The Anatomy of Canals, Anthony Burton and Derek Pratt, Tempus Publishing 2001.

The Changing Face of Kidlington Book 1, Julie Kennedy, Boyd Publications 2001.
A History of Kidlington, Valerie Offord, British Publishing Co. Ltd. 1989.
A History of Oxfordshire, Mary Jessup, Phillimore & Co. Ltd 1975.
Ladbroke, Local publication, 1995.
Out and About From Oxford, Helen Turner, Oxford Books.
Roof Off Fenny Compton, W.H. Stubbings, Warwickshire Rural Community Council.
Southam Through The Centuries, Brian Townsend, Warwickshire Books 1991.
Three Oxfordshire Parishes, B. Stapleton, Oxford Historical Society, 1893.
Tracks Through Time: A Short History of Tackley an Oxfordshire Village, Jenny Harrington, Tackley Local History Group, 1995.
Valley of the Cherwell: It's People and Places, Peter Deeley.
Warwickshire Place Names, Anthony Poulton-Smith, Countryside Books 1996.

Locally Produced Food

www.bigbarn.co.uk – the UK's main site for locally produced food.

Transport

www.oxfordshire.gov.uk/index/ environment_and _travel/travel/ publictransport/localbuses/ cherwellbuses.htm – Oxfordshire County Council summary of bus services.
www.oxfordshire.gov.uk/cyclemaps – Oxfordshire cycleways.
www.warwickshire.gov.uk/corporate/ BusTime.nsf – Warwickshire County Council summary of bus services.
www.warwickshire.gov.uk/countryside – Warwickshire walks and cycleways.
www.stagecoach-oxford.co.uk – details of main buses.
Sustrans Information Service, PO Box 21, Bristol BS99 2HA (0117 929 0888) www.sustrans.org.uk

Other

The British Horse Society, Stoneleigh Deer Park, Kenilworth, Warks CV8 2XZ (08701 202244).

INDEX

Tempus is keen to keep these guides as up to date as possible. If you have any suggestions for inclusion in the next edition of this guide, or would like to point out any changes since it was written, please email us at towpathguides@tempus-publishing.com

If you are interested in purchasing other books published by Tempus, or in case you have difficulty finding any Tempus books in your local bookshop, you can also place orders directly through our website

www.tempus-publishing.com